Marriage has changed in many ways and has caused a shift toward a worldly interpretation, having lost its spiritual values. It's like sugar that has lost its sweetness, and like music without good-sounding harmony.

THE
REASONABILITY
OF
MARRIAGE
IN A
CHANGING
WORLD

DR. ANDERSON HENRY RUFFIN

Dr. Anderson Henry Ruffin/BookBaby Publishing
7905 North Route 130
Pennsauken, NJ 08110
www.bookbaby.com

Publisher's Note: The book will focus on "covenant marriage" and share views of traditional and contemporary principles of marriage in a changing world. It will focus on the views of marriage in the United States of America, through traditional life standards and develop practices. The book will offer an assortment of writing, questioning, and critical thinking about the essence of covenant marriage as God has created it.

The Reasonability of Marriage In A Changing World/Dr. Anderson Henry Ruffin

Print ISBN: 978-1-54398-535-1
eBook ISBN: 978-1-54398-536-8

CONTENTS

ACKNOWLEDGEMENTS

I am grateful to my family and friends for giving ideas which enabled the origination of this book, and the understanding during the time of research and writing. I thank those who shared their time, emotions, and knowledge with me because they believed doing so would make a difference. Their input, support, and interest kept me going. I appreciate and acknowledge their contributions and support.

Special thanks to all who inspired me along the journey. Dr. Charles L. Lett and Dr. Aaron Dobynes (fathers in the ministry), Dr. Liz Cotton and Dr. Allam Baaheth Mentors), Robert C. Hudson (ministry/teacher), Carolyn Flanagan Ruffin (wife), Tyra, Taylor, Andrell and Thanya Ruffin (son and family), Arissa Ruffin (daughter), Jeff Ruffin (brother), Julia Ruffin (sister-in-law), Frank Ruffin (uncle), Clementine and Joe Johnson (friend and cousin), Kaitlyn Dyson, Jennifer and Eddy Dyson (family friends).

They willingly sacrificed their time, contributed resources, intelligence, patience, encouragement, and motivation during the challenging times of engagement in the writing of this book: All these beautiful people shared my desire to pass knowledge and wisdom to the present generation and especially to my granddaughters.

The sacrifices and offering of prayers enabled me to complete this book to God's glory and for the advancement of His Kingdom.

My intention in drafting this book is to pass on the blessings of a godly marriage. To God be all praises and glory for giving me the strength and patience to complete this book.

INTRODUCTION

Society once based its actions on Christian absolute values built on biblical principles. Christian absolutes are those truths and standards of Scriptures which cannot change. They are becoming less affirmative and less practical in the world today. We have marginalized (if not outlawed) Christianity in public places. Society now bases its beliefs on relative moralities that are designed to alter some values and have decided to accept that a person can do what he or she likes and is answerable to only themselves.

Most people knew what was right and wrong. Some behaviors were sinful. In recent years, more and more people are rejecting God and have come to the recognition of barring Him from society. Not only have some people attempted to get rid of God, but they have also eliminated God from their consciences by changing Christian absolutes.

Covenant marriage has been the central figure in the existence of humanity. The creation of the institution of marriage is from God. Any humanistic attempts to destroy marriage will immediately fail in any effort to depart from the original plan of God.

Major cultural shifts are occurring in every arena of life (music, philosophy, art, education, technology, entertainment, business, government, religion, spirituality, etc.). We're living in a post-national, post-rational, post-literal, post-scientific, post-technological, post-sexual, post-racial, post-human, post-traumatic, post-therapeutic, post-ethical, post-institutional, and a post-Christian era.

In public places, Christian symbols, the Bible, prayer in public school have been removed, and laws on same-sex marriage have been passed to give constitutional rights in an area once considered taboo, unthinkable, and ridiculous. Currently, we are changing the foundation of God's word to meet man's licentious desires through the government, the courts, and the education system. The goal is to invade the Church and tear down old traditional practices of moral ethics

The unbelievers have compromised God's word on covenant marriage, and it has become unethical. The gates of hell will never prevail against covenant marriage. Peter's confession of Christ reveals, "And Jesus answered and said unto him, "Blessed art thou, Simon Barjona: for flesh and blood hath not revealed it unto thee, but my Father which is in heaven. And I say also unto thee, that thou art Peter, and upon this rock I will build my church; and the gates of hell shall not prevail against it. And I will give unto thee the keys of the kingdom of heaven: and whatsoever thou shalt bind on earth shall be bound in heaven: and whatsoever thou shalt loose on earth shall be loosed in heaven" (Matt. 16:17–19). The gates of hell will never prevail against the Church and covenant marriage.

Satan is attacking the sanity of covenant marriage more than any other institution in society. Satan is trying to get us to toss out God's plan for marriage, from the beginning, and incorporates man's desirable appetite for engineering new truthful absolutes. Satan has kidnapped humanity in principle and is holding us hostage. God's final answer to this saga will be judgment and destruction like in the days of Noah.

Jesus came down to a devilish world to die for the sins of humanity and to restore God's moral foundation to avoid such a catastrophe. Humanity must become yet again ethical, consecrated, sanctified, and holy. We must get God's plan of covenant marriage back in control and restored to its place of prominence. Fake president, fake lawyers, fake news, counterfeit churches, and phony marriages shall pass away. "Heaven and earth shall pass away, but my words shall not pass away" (Matt. 24:35). God's plan for marriage will never pass away.

Many are questioning, how do you know Bible principles on marriage are true? Did marriage come from God? If so, why did He create it? How do you know that God exists? Why can't I have my view of marriage? The Bible is an account of God's historical truths concerning the meaning of marriage. Nowhere does it support same-sex marriage to animals, and things like cars. God's plan for marriage is between a male and a female. God is the author of marriage established in Genesis. "The LORD God caused a deep sleep to fall upon Adam, and he slept: and he took one of his ribs, and closed up the flesh instead thereof; and the rib, which the LORD God had taken from man, made he a woman, and brought her unto the man. Adam said, this is now bone of my bones, and flesh of my flesh: she shall be called woman, because she was taken out of man. Therefore, shall a man leave his father and his mother, and shall cleave unto his wife: and they shall be one flesh. And they were both naked, the man and his wife, and were not ashamed" (Gen. 2:21–25). The Bible contains God's clarification of covenant marriage when we have strayed away from the normal. Same-sex marriage is just the words of men but not the word of God.

Marriage has changed in many ways and shifted toward a worldly interpretation and has lost its spiritual values, and it's like sugar that has lost its sweetness, and like music without good-sounding harmony. It is vital that the institution of marriage reestablish its claim on God's authoritative approach. The same bees no longer make the honey.

"Humanity has become double-minded about marriage. A double minded man is unstable in all his ways" (James 1:8) Christians are warned not to compromise with the world on principles. A society that is double-minded will carry a heavy burden of the gravity of sin and will cause them to become blunted toward the distresses, pain, and sufferings. "Finally, brethren, whatsoever things are true, whatsoever things are honest, whatsoever things are just, whatsoever things are pure, whatsoever things are lovely, whatsoever things are of good report; if there be any virtue, and if there be any praise, think on these things. Those things, which ye have both learned, and received, and heard, and seen in me, do, and the God of peace shall be with you" (Phil. 4:8–9). The patterns of our lives are set in remembering the Creator all the days of your marriage.

CHAPTER ONE

A Descriptive View of Marriage

Some folks have become social deviants. Christians are accepting their deviant behavior, and these people have created a religious conflict rooted against the biblical principles of covenant marriage. The ideological practices have created an epidemic of disbelief and mistrust in the Bible and God's plan for marriage. Some people are letting these unethical norms set up camp in their heart and minds, and many are walking away from the original intentions God has for marriage.

Today's marriage viewpoints, perceptions, and descriptions have changed from a biblical perspective to a humanistic view. Covenant marriage is under siege! Unbiblical views are infiltrating our culture and creating a different mindset. Covenant marriage, as it used to be, is disappearing, and humans are creating its model as if there has never been another. The argument or excuses of society is that the government guarantees individual unalienable rights, but in its fullest essence has caused decay in morality and created their relative virtues.

Covenant marriage is a beacon of light for humanity to be fruitful and to produce offspring. When the family began, God was the first to officiate and ordain marriage. "Therefore, shall a man leave his father and his mother, and shall cleave unto his wife: and they shall be one flesh. And they were both naked, the man and his wife, and were not ashamed" (Gen. 2:24–25). Every man who loves a woman, and every woman who loves a man, hopes and dreams that they will find someone to share their companionship forever. Marriage is a covenant sealed by God's authority. His authority is of a state alone; while that state has jurisdiction, it is complete authority. In the beginning, God created male and female for this purpose. Therefore, God is sovereign in marriage. *Sovereign* comes from a Latin word meaning "super." It conveys the idea of superior and supreme in all ways. God is autonomous, self-directed, self-controlled, infinite in His capacities and capabilities to surpass the school of any human reasoning. God can do what he wants to do, and by any way to accomplish it. He is the best maker of marriages, combining hearts into one union. He is not the maker of same-sex marriage, or marriage with animals or things.

Anyone who chooses to make any part of creation, animate or inanimate, is not his sovereign right. "Let us therefore come boldly unto the throne of grace, that we may obtain mercy, and find grace to help in time of need" (Heb. 4:16).

Covenant marriage has broken down and turns away from the ordination God created. It has moved into a new dimension and has taken on an earthly revelation. Marriage is disappearing from traditional institutions and reestablishing its claim against a scriptural approach to instigating models without restraints or conviction. The expression of marriage introduces challenges for those who willfully engage. Marriage is not a social institution we can take or leave, as we see fit. It is not an ancient custom but is a divinely created bond between a man and a woman together in a God-ordained, lifelong relationship.

What does the Bible say about marriage? The Bible says that marriage is God's ideal, "And the LORD God caused a deep sleep to fall upon Adam, and he slept: and he took one of his ribs, and closed up the flesh instead thereof, and the rib, which the LORD God had taken from man, made he a woman, and brought her unto the man. Adam said, this is now bone of my bones, and flesh of my flesh: she shall be called woman, because she was taken out of man. Therefore, shall a man leave his father and his mother, and shall cleave unto his wife: and they shall be one flesh" (Gen. 2:21–24). God is the owner of marriage because He initiated its formation. God is the architect of marriage and He is the contractor who erected the design on a stable foundation.

Covenant marriage is a permanent plan between male and female. "For this reason, a man will leave his father and mother and be united to his wife, and the two will become one flesh? So, they are no longer two, but one flesh. Therefore, what God has joined together, let no one separate" (Matt. 19:6). Ideally, only death should dissolve a marriage. "The wife hath not power of her own body, but the husband: and likewise, also the husband hath not power of his own body, but the wife" (1 Cor. 7). In marriage, the husband and wife belong to each other). Marriage is based on the principles of love. "Husbands love your wives, even as Christ also loved the church, and gave himself for it" (Eph. 5:25). Marriage is a living symbol of Christ and the Church. "Therefore, as the church is subject unto Christ, so let the wives be to their own husbands in everything" (Eph. 5:24). It is right and honorable. "Marriage is honorable in all, and the bed undefiled: but whoremongers and adulterers God will judge" (Heb. 13:4). In marriage, each partner has responsibilities in caring for the other. "Husbands, in the same way be considerate as you live with your wives and treat them with respect as the weaker partner and as heirs with you of the gracious gift of life, so that nothing will hinder your prayers" (1 Pet. 3:7).

We live in a society that always has operated under Christian principles which cannot be altered. Humanity has begun to tolerate devious behavior or relative morality resulting in a fundamental shift in redefining marriage. How has this come to be? Some people have attempted to eliminate God's mind on the issue of same-sex marriage. Some individuals have tried to erase God from society by changing the laws to accommodate their ideas and values based on man-created absolutes. Behaviors such as homosexuality, pornography, abortion, and sexual deviancy that were considered impractical are now acceptable. Years ago, marriage had some Christian absolutes. People knew what was right and wrong about marriage. Most people accepted and respect the belief of God about marriage. In recent decades, marriage behavior has changed. More and more people are rejecting Jehovah God's principles of marriage.

The definition of marriage has become highly controversial. Dictionaries cannot resolve the issue. The controversy involves cultural traditions, religious beliefs, legal rulings, and ideas about fairness and fundamental human rights. The critical point of marriage dispute has to do with marriage between two people of the same sex, often referred to as same-sex marriage or gay marriage. Same-sex marriages are now recognized by law and are growing in countries around the world. Same-sex marriage was legally validated throughout the United States by the Supreme Court's decision in Obergefell vs. Hodges in 2015. In many other parts of the world, marriage continues between a man and woman, but that is rapidly changing.

Therefore, the definition of marriage according to man is broad enough to encompass marriage between male and female, marriage between the same gender, and with animals and things. These types of marriages are currently recognized in varying cultures, places, religions, and systems of law. The essence of marriage is the joining of husband and wife to become one flesh in a covenant relationship. The joining may be invisible to man, but it is authentic to God.

Redefining marriage in the law is endangering religious freedom. Those who stand for traditional marriage are already being called bigots. We are facing false charges of discrimination or hatred against same-sex marriage. People have been punished for acting on their religious belief in traditional marriage. Christians are to protect the meaning of covenant marriage because stable marriages and family life are the foundation of a flourishing society.

Christians have suffered being sued, lost their jobs, and been forced to close the doors to their businesses (florists, photographers, bakers, etc.). Schools, hospitals, charitable institutions are threatened and have lost access to public funds, non-profit status, or licenses to operate. Policies have already occurred to accommodate privileges and care for couples of same-sex marriages because of their contemporary views of marriage.

We now look at nations that recognize a relationship between two men, two women, a man and a dog or man and a car. Sharon Tendler, December 2005, a 41-year-old eccentric British millionaire, married a dolphin named Cindy at an Israeli resort. Joseph Guiso, a 20-year-old Australian man, December 2010, married his best friend, a five-year-old Labrador. A man marries a steam engine train, a video game character, and a Barbie doll. A woman marries the Berlin Wall, a roller coaster, the Eiffel Tower, and a pillow.

The freedom of same-sex marriages created opposition to a procreative position and invoked charges against biblical exegeses to support claims that marriage is strictly defined as not between male and female. Some enthusiast has created religious conflict rooted in the issue of human-made devices that is not biblical and logical has launched a battle for men's souls in a culture more and more becoming non-Christian. Whatever diseases are fueling the epidemic, they are infecting society, the younger generation, and the continued existence of humanity.

Biblical marriage is a great institution, and same-sex marriage wants to become the norm. Marriage is the most hallowed of all earthly institutions. A complete trust in godly principles is one of the most significant enriching factors in preserving godly marriage. In recent years, it has been under extensive scrutiny. We are turning to a melancholy that is far removing ourselves from the spiritual.

We are living in times when the world is attacking the absolutes, and in the days to come, the world is contending to destroy the traditional doctrines of marriage that were delivered to Adam and Eve. There is no combination of power which can destroy marriage except the power of man within an attempt to remove God, who is the Author and Finisher of marriage. The biblical view of marriage should be viewed as one-dimensional, culturally absolute.

Contemporary marriage has gained personal status while it conflicts with the plan of God. Many people share the belief that it is okay to embrace a freedom of choice. We are living in a fast-paced, fast-moving, ever-changing world. Therefore, I believe it is nonsense to oppose God's view of covenant marriage.

Today we have many who are involved in traditional marriage and have discovered excitement and encouragement because they are courageous witnesses of the truth God establish. Marriage seems to be in a state of despair and frustration. Indeed, there needs to be much more sympathy and understanding for those who have experienced the great tragedy of same-sex marriage and whose lives can be reversed. For covenant marriage, there is still much to be hoped for and expected in terms of fulfillment and happiness in life. Have you forgotten the blessing of God in your covenant marriage, the benefits that will last until death separate you?

Society has come to some agreement that it is okay to dishonor the edicts of God. Covenant marriage has proved its value during my years of marriage. It is presently meeting stiff opposition from outside forces attacking the foundation of marriage with the desires to engage in same-sex marriage, technology support, homosexuality, gender theory, the attack on parental rights, atheism, and social media platform.

Once upon a time, we received news in traditional formats from finite media sources by way of newspapers, television, and radio. The formats have changed. Twitter rejects Craig Stellpflug, a former pastor, requesting an advertising platform to use this social media site to promote his new book advocating traditional Christian belief in marriage titled *One Man One Woman: God's Original Design for Marriage*, published by WestBow Press. The evils of social media are exposing ideas of marriage that are unjust, ideas about casual sex, sexuality in sitcom shows, movies, and support cohabitation before marriage. Walter Cronkite closed his CBS nightly newscast saying, "And that's the way it is," meaning those are the facts.

Today, we have concluded that if a person "lusts" for something enough, we ought to let them have it. A man "lusts" for naked women – click on an internet picture. A person "lusts" for a high, we legalized marijuana. A person "lusts" for someone they're not married to; and the behavior become accepted. A person "lusts" for someone of the same sex; we have legalized same-sex marriage. A person "lusts" to become a gender they were not born as; we think they ought to be allowed to change. Humanity's lust has become extremely ambiguous without motives. There are no limits to what humanity will lust after. Anything that might seem "forbidden" is something that some people have the greatest desire for.

Some people are enjoying the spotlight challenging biblical marriage. They seem confused, and lack understanding and appreciation for God's plan for marriage. Contemporary marriage experiences are different from my mom and dad's. They believed getting married in the Church was sacred. Most marriages today are not sacred when it involves the same sex, with things and animals. It has become the norm against God's plan.

The purpose of dealing with the dangers of marriage is to warn those who would enter marriage casually, without serious consideration of the consequences of their decisions. When a couple takes the oath of marriage, they make a vow, a vow which they're obligated to keep for life.

Marriage, then, has an integrally biblical dimension. It is the foundation of the family, the fundamental unit in society, where human sexuality is regulated toward the finality of new human life, where citizens learn how to live responsibly and engage in the family and community. The union is not merely a cultural or historical reality, but rather, an ultimate manifestation of what it means to be human. After all, only human beings and not animals or things unite as husband or wife. Children develop their personality and gender identity through the family created within the institution of a covenant marriage.

John Hardon, the author of *Pocket Catholic Dictionary*, explains four elements common to natural marriage throughout history.

1. It is a union of opposite sexes (male and female).

2. It is a lifelong union, ending only with the death of one spouse.

3. It excludes a union with any other person so long as the marriage exists.

4. Its lifelong and exclusiveness are guaranteed by contract.

Today, marriage has its moments of imperfection as the seasons change. There is a need to continue teaching sound doctrine, fashioning godly minds in a contemporary society. When we dishonor God's plan for marriage, Satan takes up arms against the institution of marriage and forms a sea of doubt. Humanity's concerns for the community are to rebuild on the principles of God. We must be willing to bear the whips and scorns of time to be successful and get covenant marriage back on solid ground.

I once met a lady, and she shared these thoughts with me. The years of loneliness and discouragement were evident in her once beautiful face. After passing a few words in conversation, she was quick to say that life had not been rich and rewarding for her and that she was tired of facing the struggle alone. I have never been married. Then came a most startling disclosure; she said, "Bad as it was, if I had to do it over again, knowing what I do now, I would have sought to marry. The worst thing that happened to me is living all these years in loneliness."

Covenant marriage contrasts sharply with same-sex marriage. Same-sex marriage relationships involve participation in non-reproductive types of acts by members of the same sex who are equal in dignity as human persons, but not complementary qua masculinity and femininity.

A same-sex couple cannot further the common good of society by creating and nurturing a new human life in a way worthy of human dignity. Underlying this approach is a view that human sexuality is not a relationship between persons of the same sex. It lacks a central component of male and female, namely, the fundamental biological participation in reproductive-type acts which are the foundation of the psychological, emotional, and moral reality of the couple.

Marriage is an expression through which the union of male and female become husband and wife and consummate to become mother and father. Lastly, while the gay community may be made up of partners who are raising children, this fact alone does not render their relationships more "marriage-like," nor does the loving aspects or long-term nature of their bond produce offspring. "God blessed them, and God said unto them, be fruitful, and multiply, and replenish the earth, and subdue it: and have dominion over the fish of the sea, and over the fowl of the air, and over every living thing that move upon the earth" (Gen. 1:28). Only male and female can complete the task.

Jesus said, "Have you not read that He who created them from the beginning made them male and female. Therefore, a man shall leave his father and his mother and hold fast to his wife, and the two shall become one flesh? So, they are no longer two but one flesh. Wherefore they are no more twain, but one flesh. What therefore God hath joined together, let not man put asunder." (Matt. 19:4–6). We can see God's desires for marriage, determined by God, and defended by God. He has joined together, let no man put asunder. A man doesn't break off all contact with his parents when he gets married. He makes new priorities to have a wife, family, and children. His wife becomes the single most important relationship in his life.

Blaine Fowers, a licensed psychologist, says, "The ultimate truths about marriage, are captivated by contemporary ideas of marriage. But the real facts make it painfully clear, and the world has got it all wrong. A godly marriage is the only foundation on which a lasting and fulfilling marriage can be built to last. "Let us pray without ceasing" (1 Thess. 5:17) for God's plan for marriage.

God's plan for marriage from the beginning is between male and female and will stand forever. Jesus tells us that marriage is a concept joined by God. "Have ye not read, that he which made them at the beginning made them male and female, and said, for this cause shall a man leave father and mother, and shall cleave to his wife: and they twain shall be one flesh?" (Matt. 19:3–9). Marriage is a relationship properly appreciated in the most delightful sacred acts of all human relations. Man needs a woman, and a woman would not exist without a man.

Marriage is a gift that the union of two as one may acquire everlasting excitement as they travel over the hills, through the valleys and plains of life's journey. It is held together when two people fall in love and tie the knot, for life. God joins an eternal union of two souls to last and to love until death do, them apart.

CHAPTER TWO

A Covenant Marriage

American culture has made marriage a constitutional right, of passage in the wrong direction. I have a growing concern that the Christian community has passively watched the "dumbing down" of the covenant marriage. Marriage has become little more than an upgraded social contract between two people, not a holy covenant between a man and a woman and their God for a lifetime.

My responsibility is to be thought-provoking and to foster a conversation around the issues of covenant marriage. It is a sensitive issue to cultivate a better understanding; we must continue to pray for those who choose to take this path in God's grace, mercy, and love.

God made a woman from the rib he had taken out of the man, and he brought her to the man. Adam said, "This is now bone of my bones, and flesh of my flesh: she shall be called woman, because she was taken out of man. Therefore, shall a man leave his father and his mother, and shall cleave unto his wife: and they shall be one flesh" (Gen. 2:23–24).

Humanity should continue to honor covenant marriage and keep the marriage bed pure, for God will judge the adulterer and all the sexual immoralities. "Marriage is honorable in all, and the bed undefiled: but whoremongers and adulterers God will judge" (Heb. 13:4). The first marriage is between Adam and Eve, and the last marriage is between Christ and His Bride. The two marriage scenes tell the story of redemption. The Bible wraps itself around marriage. God's people need to prepare spiritually for covenant marriage. The prophet says, "Yet ye say, Wherefore? Because the LORD hath been witness between thee and the wife of thy youth, against whom thou hast dealt treacherously: yet is she thy companion, and the wife of thy covenant" (Mal. 2:14).

The Scriptures define a covenant marriage as a binding relationship which is meant to last a lifetime. It does not deal with the signing of a so-called contract, but instead with emphasis on biblical truths and is made with a covenant keeping God. Humanity has lost the biblical truth regarding covenant marriage.

Marriage is no longer in step with religious beliefs but has changed to keep pace with a fast-moving, ever-changing technology world. These are the times when the world is attacking absolute values, that in the latter days to come, the evil spirits of the world are contending to destroy Christian doctrines of marriage that were upheld by our ancestors.

Marriage is not an emotional satisfaction of two individuals, but is for the good of humanity, which stands under the blessing and the curse of God. Societies that put individual fulfillment before the principles of God will soon give way to a multitude of addictions, deep corruptions, and ultimately, collapse. God will judge any nation that institutes same-sex marriage.

A covenant marriage involves a walk until death do you part. "Whoso find a wife find a good thing and obtain favor of the LORD" (Prov. 18:22). It produces a divine oneness between a male and a female in union. Two hearts are prepared to become one until the end. For this cause, a man should leave his mother, his father, cleave to his wife, and they become one flesh. Wherefore they are no more separate (meaning two), but they are one flesh. When you are married, God sees both of you and neither of you. God sees both of you and neither of you because you are one.

Marriage may also be described like making mashed potatoes. The individual potatoes are skinned alive and thrown into hot water. They stay there and sweat it out together in the intense heat. Then the cook takes a metal masher and crushes them together until you can't tell one from the other. They look alike, they talk alike, and they taste alike and act alike. God says, "And they twain shall be one flesh: so, then they are no more twain, but one flesh. What therefore God hath joined together, let not man put asunder" (Mark 10:9). The sexual union seals the covenant.

A covenant marriage relationship begins long before the couple gets to the altar. The couple needs to become aware of their responsibilities. We have too many men and women running headlong to the altar trying to find the person, the one, the soulmate of their dream. Running headlong to the altar, they have no idea of a covenant marriage relationship.

Some men approach the altar of marriage with foolish ideas. I knew you were going to be my wife. God told me you were going to be my soulmate; the first time I saw your face. I find it funny that some will say, "I heard from God you were going to be my wife," but in other areas of your life God's name is never mentioned. Many make comments with stable clarity that focus on romantic decisions. There is something wrong with this kind of lingo in your heart and mind. Women have heard that story repeatedly from men. It is because we don't understand what the altar of marriage represents.

The world is trying to take the altar of covenant marriage away from the truth. But I'm reclaiming it back today based on the word of God. I want us to understand what this thing called covenant marriage is all about. A covenant marriage is the linking of two chains, the blending of sugar and salt, and the union of two hearts walking together through life to meet the rising sun daily. Together they bear life's burdens, discharging their duties, sharing joy and sorrows. A covenant marriage is more than moonlight, roses, candy, and puppy love. It is much more than the singing of sweet love songs, the whispering of the love poems, and vows of undying affections.

What makes a marriage enriching? Having a companionship and enjoying the fruits of your labor anchor on having the presence of God and the Holy Spirit to produce the kernel.

First, we must understand what an altar is, from a biblical approach. An altar in the Old Testament was a table-like structure. It was a place where someone came to bring an offering, such as sacrifice to God. Genesis 8:20 tells us, Noah was the first to erect an altar. That place was consecrated and made sacred. At that moment you approached the altar, it commemorated an encounter with God that had a profound impact upon someone.

Whatever was going on was declared sacred at that moment. Today, most cathedrals, houses of worship have an altar. In some places, it may be a stage or an elevated platform. The worshipper would come to the altar to engage in sacred reverence: prayer, communion, weddings, and for other holy purposes.

When you come to the marriage altar, you need to know what is implicit. The altar was a place of sacrifice. "Noah built an altar unto the LORD; and took of every clean beast, and of every clean fowl, and offered burnt offerings on the altar. And the LORD smelled a sweet savor; and the LORD said in his heart, I will not again curse the ground any more for man's sake; for the imagination of man's heart is evil from his youth; neither will I again smite any more everything living, as I have done" (Gen. 8:20–21). Now when you come to the altar of marriage, it is a moment of sacrificing something. When you stand, you begin with the mentality of getting something, but you need to give something rather than obtain.

Too many people come to the marriage altar looking at their spouse thinking about what they are to receive and get out of the relationship. Some individuals believe that they are obtaining a spouse to help them pay the bills, they have a venue for legal sex and someone to keep their life from boredom. Nobody is coming to the altar with an understanding; this is a place where I must give. "In process of time it came to pass, that Cain brought of the fruit of the ground an offering unto the LORD. And Abel, he also brought of the firstlings of his flock and of the fat thereof. And the LORD had respect unto Abel and to his offering, but unto Cain and to his offering he had not respect" (Gen. 4:3–4). In a covenant marriage, the bride and groom at the altar are offering themselves to the Lord.

An altar is a place of sacrifice where you give God your best. You don't give Him secondhand stuff. When you come to the mar- riage altar, you surrender something. You surrender some rights, independence, time, money, and energy to God and your spouse. One day, you will find out it is a disaster because you are unwilling to make a sacrifice. If you are not ready, don't get married.

A marriage altar is a place of sacrifice and submission God called Abraham to sacrifice his only son, Isaac. He was to become the father of many nations. Isaac was a seed through which this promise was to come. Then God turns around and asks Abraham to sacrifice his only son. He packed up and with his son, he marched to the place where he was directed to make the sacrifice. I could only imagine what a father felt like taking that walk to give up what he treasured the most. Abraham must have felt appalling when Isaiah said, "My father: and he said, "Here am I, my son. And he said,

Behold the fire and the wood: but where is the lamb for a burnt offering?" (Gen. 22:7). Abraham lifted the knife to take his son's life before God intervened and provided a way out with a ram caught in the bushes. Abraham was committed to making a sacrifice to God, despite the cost.

When you come to the altar, you come with an attitude of submission. Covenant marriage is a relationship of mutual submission. Ephesians 5:21, says, "Submitting yourselves one to another in the fear of God." Most men like this Scripture, "For the husband is the head of the wife, even as Christ is the head of the church" (Eph. 5:25). This Scripture is presented in the wrong way. If the husband does not submit to his wife, there is chaos. There is total submission between the husband and wife. There will be times when you give to the other person like Christ gave himself for the Church. You submit to each other and to Christ. Abraham fully surrendered to God. Here is the great thing you see in the story; God will provide. You must fully surrender to God and your spouse in a covenant marriage.

Check out the patterns of submission. If they do not have a habit of submitting to other people growing up as an adult, they will not submit to you in marriage. You need to know the individual you are going to marry has people that have authority and can speak into their life. You need to know who they are. You need to meet them and sit down and ask questions about the person's character. You need to know if they have godly values, know if they are reliable and if they have not committed any crimes or are wanted by law enforcement. Can you give me two instances where this person I'm thinking about marrying wanted to go left, but you said go right? You said that's not the place you need to go, and they still went left.

If the person you are seeking to marry don't have a pattern of submission, someday they will not listen to you, or submit to you.

You will be powerless to do anything in their life. In some cases, a spouse will be sitting in a chair alone, trying to get some help to make the marriage grow because their partner doesn't want to come to counseling. Who in their life can you appeal to, to gain a relational level and call them to account? Nobody. Somebody that does not have a pattern of willingness to submit to authority in their life will never do it in your situation.

If you do not have a life pattern of submission to God, you are never going to submit to your spouse. You need to see a pattern of submission to God; it's not about you. It's about God's will in your life, and you surrender to God. Then you will surrender to your wife. You need to practice a pattern of submission throughout your marriage. An altar is a place of sacrifice and it is a place of submission.

An altar is also a place of service. The fire on the altar must be kept burning continuously. "The fire shall ever be burning upon the altar; it shall never go out" (Lev. 6:13). The altar of marriage is a day in and day out continuous service. You must continuously serve your wife. You must keep loving your wife. When you continually serve your wife, you keep the fire on the altar burning. When you stop serving your wife, the light begins to dwindle. There are marriages today where there is no fire burning. There are barely embers with a little bit of smoke coming out. When the two decide to stop serving, the light eventually goes out. An altar is a place of service. If you don't like to serve, don't get married. If you are a selfish person, it's going to be challenging to become an unselfish person after you get married. A covenant marriage is about service to your spouse.

The person you marry needs to have a pattern of service in their life. Maybe he/she can't see the big picture because they want you to serve them all the time. You need to know that he/she has a servant's heart before you get married. Because this is the only way, you will be convinced before going into a marriage that they will serve you. They are serving you because they are getting what they want at that time. They need to show a pattern of service before you get married.

God made a covenant with Abraham saying, "Unto thy seed have I given this land, from the river of Egypt unto the great river, the river Euphrates" (Gen. 15:18). The LORD God testified, "And I will remember my covenant, which is between me and you and every living creature of all flesh; and the waters shall no more become a flood to destroy all flesh. And the bow shall be in the cloud; and I will look upon it, that I may remember the everlasting covenant between God and every living creature of all flesh that is upon the earth" (Gen. 9:15–16). It is the power of the covenant maker that keeps the agreement enforced. God passed through himself, and he said this one is on me. It was binding forever.

What did this look like? A shadow of two people making a blood covenant where there was no escape, no rule breakers, and you were stuck. Down the middle of the animals was holy ground. The two individuals would walk through the middle of these animals, meeting in the middle. A pathway allowed the two people to walk between the carcass, solemnizing the promise saying, "May God do so to me [cut me in half] if I ever break this covenant with you and God!" They would cut the right palm of their hands so that they were bleeding and would join hands to make a blood covenant together. They would share vows of commitment and possessions they were giving to one another. Then they would take off their coats and exchange them between them. After they exchanged coats and belts, they would take a portion of the person's name and make it a part of their name. They would depart from that place.

A blood covenant was irrevocable without an escape clause. In the Old Testament days, a marriage covenant was solemn and binding. When two people entered a promise of marrying, a goat or lamb would be slain, and the carcass would be cut in half and separated on the ground. A covenant in ancient days had more substance than today. Covenants were not easily broken with minor penalties. A covenant terminates at the death of one of the parties.

What does a covenant have to do with marriage? When a man marries a virgin, the rupture of the hymen is a symbol of the shedding of blood, which is an indication of purity. It is the seal of the covenant, and it is binding for life. A marriage was sealed by the shedding of a virgin's blood during her first sexual experience with her husband. Did Eve bleed on her wedding night? Only she and Adam knew, but we don't know. There is no reason for Eve to have experienced that pain before she sinned. The Bible doesn't give us an answer until after the couple sinned. The curse brought pain to childbearing and all it entails. We don't teach today that a woman must offer a sacrifice of blood to seal her marriage.

Many people have sexual sins that they must ask forgiveness prior to marriage. I would consider them to be virgins. Are their marriages less valid than others? Do we live under a covenant of purity in marriage? We live under a covenant of grace with forgiveness and mercy.

When you enter a covenant with your beloved, the sign is usually a ring, which serves as a constant reminder (memorial) of the solemnity and binding of your marriage covenant. A covenant marriage has become little more than an upgraded social contract between two people, a man and a woman.

The wedding altar has a significant meaning. The altar is where the bride and groom meet to regurgitate some sweet words, kiss, and ride off into the sunset. The wedding altar has deep spiritual symbolism. The wedding altar and ceremony are symbolic of the blood covenant of the Old Testament. Most couples do not look at the wedding day and realize the symbolism of the wedding. The groom enters first into the chapel. He is positioned to look down the middle of the aisle, a pathway between the rows of seats. A white runner down the middle aisle is placed to symbolize holiness and purity of the path.

In the New Testament, Ephesians 5, Paul describes that the relationship of the husband and wife is symbolic of the relationship of Jesus (the groom) and the Church (the bride). The groom looks down the middle of the altar and calls to himself the bride. His bride comes down, usually escorted by the father. The mother and father of the groom and bride are seated in the front row because they are a vital part of the wedding decision. They were the ones who made the final decision on whether their son or daughter was to marry. Some of you, if you had listened to your parents about whom you were to marry, would have saved yourself some heartaches.

The wedding ceremony itself was symbolic of the Old Testament blood covenant. The bride comes down to the groom wearing a veil. In the Old Testament temple, there was a veil that separated the presence of God from the people. When Jesus died on Calvary, the cover was torn apart, giving the people access into the presence of God. So, when the bride lifts her veil, she is giving her groom access. Then the ceremony stops. Usually, the minister would turn them toward each other. Sometimes they will join their right hand together, symbolizing the blood covenant. They share some vows of committing to what they are giving up. Then they exchange some rings. The ring is an unbroken circle, much like the belts that were exchanged in the blood covenant. The minister allows them to kiss; that's so sweet. The minister turns them toward the audience for the pronouncement and presentation of this couple who now have a new identity with a shared name together, just like in the blood covenant. They become a part of each other's name and walk away together.

A covenant marriage of today needs to reflect God's plan for a covenant marriage. That's what marriage is supposed to be about today. We have turned it into a show and all kinds of extra stuff when taking the marriage vows. But it's supposed to be a covenant of marriage you are making when you stepped to the altar. The wedding covenant is a perfect mirror of God's blood covenant in the Old Testament. What that means is marriage comes at a high price. We don't understand that when you meet God at the altar, he intends to do something in you. So that when you receive God promise at the altar, you are committed to allowing transformation in your married lives. That's what's supposed to be happening at the altar. It was a wedding covenant at the altar. So now we have clarity.

When you come to the altar, you have already decided in your heart to point to a place of sacrifice, to submit and to serve your spouse. Let's say it a little differently. When you come to the altar, you are coming to a place where your spouse looks at you and says I am going to sacrifice, submit, and serve you until death do us part.

The man and woman individually decide when they are ready to marry and whom they desire to marry. They must choose one another if these two will become one. The technical term for this process is called "cathexis." Cathexis is an investment of mental or emotional energy in a person, object, or idea. When we apply this process in preparation to marriage based on love (agape), each party decides to help one another to be winners in their pursuit of all their innate needs and not merely their sexual urges. Although each party in the marriage loves themselves, they are at the same time extending their ego boundaries to include their spouse. The young man and woman decide to replace the word *love* in this Scripture with their own "self" before their marriage. Marriage based on God's quality of love requires mature, integrated individuals.

The wedding is a grand occasion, creating a covenant between two recipients, as printed in *The Book of Common Prayer*:

Groom: I John Doe, takes thee, Jane Doe, to be my wedded wife, to have and to hold from this day forward, for better for worse, for richer or poorer, in sickness and in health, to love and to cherish, till death we do part, according to God's holy ordinance; and to that, I plight thee my troth (promise to give loyalty, and faithfulness).

Bride: I, Jane Doe, take thee, John Doe, to be my married husband, to have and to hold from this day forward, for better for worse, for richer or poorer, in sickness and in health, to love, cherish, and to obey, till death we do part, according to God's holy ordinance; and to that, I give thee my troth.

Dr. Fred Lowery, the author of *Covenant Marriage,* asks a question; is your marriage a covenant or a contract? A covenant marriage involves a relationship of trust from that day forward in any condition. You have given up your rights to meet your spouse's needs. You promise to put your spouse's interest before your interest until death do you part. The parties trust each other and put no limits on their responsibility. A contract marriage is an agreement based on restrictions and limits on carrying out the duties.

What are the differences between a covenant marriage and marriage that incorporates human intervention (same-sex, marriage to animals and things)?

- Both invite and initiate a response and create a relationship.

- A covenant marriage is guarded by grace and oath, so the essence is the consent that God bound them in the relationship. The other is bound by human inventiveness.

- A covenant marriage is based on an obligation in faith to God, and the other can only justified faith through social initiatives.

- A covenant marriage includes promises to God, between a male and female, and the other makes promises to animals and things.

- Covenant marriage requires sacrifices between a male and female, and the other a continuous relationship to animals or things.

You marry because you discover the love of your life. Two imperfect people get married and promise a commitment to provide, protect, and live together for life. God's plan is for one woman and one man to commit to each other exclusively and permanently. Commitment builds up faith and develops character. It is a spiritual discipline requiring time, work, and determination.

In a covenant marriage, selfishness has no right, but in this modern culture, the demands are so high that many partners are overshadowed with someone becoming selfish (you want the best in all situations for you). Your good is what is important to you. You can do this yourself without any help. Selfishness will destroy any marriage when a spouse is looking to his/her interests but not to the benefits of each other (Phil. 2:4).

In a non-Christian marriage, one partner may only exist to serve, share, listen, submit to his happiness. Two contrasting attitudes may exist between a contract and covenant marriage, as described in the following chart from Dr. Fred Lowery recent book, *Covenant Marriage*:

The Contract Marriage Attitudes

- You better do it!
- What do I get?
- What will it take?
- It's not my responsibility.

- It's not my fault.
- I'll meet you halfway.
- I'll be faithful for now.
- I am suspicious.
- I must.
- It's a deal.

The Covenant Marriage Attitudes

- How may I serve you?
- What can I give?
- Whatever does it take?
- I'm happy to do it!
- I accept responsibility.
- I'll give 100 percent.
- I'll be faithful forever.
- I am trusting.
- I want to.
- It's a relationship.

After the wedding vows, it is time to drop ego boundaries and become one in the marriage bed. Let the young man or woman beware while choosing a mate. The institution of marriage, though troubled by our hardened hearts, was initially designed by God to manifest His image and to provide stability for society and safe handling for each generation to arrive and thrive on the earth. In the act of marriage, the male and female may achieve the reproduction of themselves by having children. To make this reproduction, the development and maintenance of a family and offspring are for the fulfillment and continuation of humanity. "Wherefore God also gave them up to uncleanness through the lusts of their own hearts, to dishonor their own bodies between themselves. Who changed the truth of God into a lie, and worshipped and served the creature more than the Creator, who is blessed forever? Amen. For this cause, God gave them up unto vile affections: for even their women did change the natural use into that which is against nature" (Rom. 1:24–27). Any other combination of the same sexes in union create sexual impurities and perversion that are biblically incorrect.

The traditional model of marriage is quickly fading. Within a few decades, the relevancy of a godly marriage is disappearing. A clash between the ideologies of a covenant marriage and contemporary modernism will cause society to disengage from active evolvement in a covenant marriage.

Contrary to Western culture, marriage is no longer recognized as a religious institution, but rather the rationalized right of those who claim a detour through the justice department and exist with the necessary rights to change the original script of marriage between a male and female.

Marriage today should be examined from the perspective of whether the union of a woman to woman or man to man makes a productive and self-fulfilled product of social expectations. If we looked at the original script, marriage is God's way of offering the opportunity to achieve an intimate relationship with the opposite sex to satisfy each of their sex drives and to produce likeness for the propagation of humans. Both partners can fulfill one another's needs for companionship.

Man needs encouragement and companionship that can be provided only from a female spouse. That's the way God made them and that's the way it should be. Jesus reaffirms when He answered, "Have ye not read, that he which made them at the beginning made

32

them male and female. And said, "For this cause shall a man leave father and mother, and shall cleave to his wife: and they twain shall be one flesh?" (Matt. 19:4–5).

Humanity has become isolated in their ego boundaries to find pleasure by sharing a covenant relationship with the same sex, with animals, and things. We suddenly drop these ego boundaries to feel comfortable. Sexual predispositions strongly motivate them. It happens to people at the time when sexual needs exceed their spiritual requirements. How can two men or two women or any other thing make babies? It is a complicated relationship and is also a perverted act. "What? Know ye not that your body is the temple of the Holy Ghost, which is in you, which ye have of God, and ye are not your own? For ye are bought with a price: therefore, glorify God in your body, and in your spirit, which are God's" (1 Cor. 19:19-20).

God has given the m perverted hearts to seek their desires. God gave them over in the sinful desires of their hearts to sexual impurity for the degrading of their bodies with one another. "For this cause, God gave them up unto vile affections: for even their women did change the natural use into that which is against nature. Likewise, also the men, leaving the natural use of the woman, burned in their lust one toward another; men with men working that which is unseemly, and receiving in themselves that recompence of their error which was meet" (Rom. 1:24–28).They exchanged the truth about God for a lie and worshiped things rather than the Creator. God gave them over to their shameful lusts. The women exchanged natural sexual relations for unnatural ones. In the same way, men also abandoned physical relationships with women and were inflamed with lust for one another. Men committed shameful acts with other men and received in themselves the due penalty for their error. Furthermore, just as they did not think it worthwhile to retain the knowledge of God, so God gave them over to a depraved mind so that they do what ought not to be done.

Everything has been ordained to operate on a system of godly laws. There are natural laws and spiritual laws that govern the universe. The atom obeyed the commandments of God when He ordered the world into existence. God put in place religious rules and principles to guide all activity. These spiritual laws work in concert with natural laws and govern the unseen spiritual reality of everything tangible to the senses. It is the existence of God's laws that require a man and woman to be holy.

God's word has been around since before time. He has seen everything that has gone on. His testimony is always right and can be counted on to be accurate. God made it clear in the beginning when only two people, one male, and one female, were designed with a purpose.

Many people in this world have difficulty understanding God's word. The misunderstanding is often used as an excuse to reject God and His authority over their lives. God created humanity with a purpose of love so intense that He died for us. But the intensity has diminished with rejection. The love that drove God to offer up His only begotten Son on the cross is extinguished when we turn our backs on His principles. It burns more brightly when humanity recognizes God's generous love for us. "Let no corrupt communication proceed out of your mouth, but that which is good to the use of edifying, that it may minister grace unto the hearers" (Eph. 4:29). "Wherefore comfort yourselves together, and edify one another, even as also ye do" (1 Thess. 5:11).

Sin has a disastrous eternal effect. Adam and Eve were the first to understand that rebellion against a loving Father separated themselves from the presence of God. We all will stand naked in the sight of God because of sin. You will abide in the shame of your lust: cut off from communion, salvation, life eternal, and the source of truth. You die and go to Hell, a place of torment forever because of your disrespect and rejection of God's spiritual laws.

God said to Adam, "Because thou hast hearkened unto the voice of thy wife, and hast eaten of the tree, of which I commanded thee, saying, Thou shalt not eat of it: cursed is the ground for thy sake; in sorrow shalt thou eat of it all the days of thy life" (Gen. 3:17). You will be cursed and separated from my presence. God put them out of the Garden of Eden to work for a living, because of disobedience, they did eat of the tree and died spiritually. God put them out and they had to cultivate (farm) the ground (world); through painful toil to eat all the days of their life.

"Beware lest any man spoil you through philosophy and vain deceit, after the tradition of men, after the rudiments of the world, and not after Christ." (Col. 2:8–10). God's warning to this present generation is, don't mess with covenant marriage. Covenant marriage has a single defining purpose between male and female joined into one flesh, a union, and to the development of children. It cannot be narrowed down to another dishonorable and meaningless intention far from the plans of God. Insisting that marriage change as the world changes would likewise weaken the purpose by making it brittle, irrelevant, or both. With an increasingly secular, indifferent, and an antagonistic mindset toward covenant marriage, Christians must do everything possible to keep the foundation of marriage secured. This union is not to be looked upon as unwise, unadvisedly or lightly, but in fear of God. It begins and ends with a proper emphasis on God.

CHAPTER THREE

The Changing Trend of Covenant Marriage

Marriage views are far beyond what they have been in previous generations. Marriage is a way of becoming a functioning member of society as a male or female ready for adulthood. The act of becoming married complies with social norms, and therefore becomes accepted. It rewards the couple in unison to start a family.

Today's views of marriage have made a radical change. The time of preparation, a time of coming together, a time of high expectation and anticipation, is no longer expected as the norm. The advent of the marriage celebration has nothing at all to do with the number of shopping days left until Christmas. It is altogether different from the coming together of two to become one.

The placement of poinsettias, lighting the first candle, dreams of a better world, and expecting visions, has nothing to do anymore with sugar-plum fairies dancing in your heads. Marriage invites us to fill the cup of a future with a full measure of tomorrow's expectations and hope for a brighter future with some. But slow leaks in the sanctifying dimension of marriage is causing marriages to become flat tires.

God's plan for marriage is to prevent immorality. "Nevertheless, to avoid fornication, let every man have his own wife, and let every woman have her own husband" (1 Cor. 7:2). Marriage is to be honorable in all and the bed undefiled (Heb. 13:4). Marriages serve as a model of a relationship with Christ. "Husbands love your wives, even as Christ also loved the church, and gave himself for it" (Eph. 3:25). God's ideal of marriage has never changed and will not change. His design is older than any of God's commandments. It is a lifetime relationship and binding commitment that is designed for life.

Humanity has developed a view of marriage that contrast with the principles of God. A lot of tension exists between humanity and God. We have developed a new institution for marriage that is going nowhere spiritually. Humanity has failed its spiritual walk in marriage. The union of male and female reminds us conveniently of God's word and God's design for marriage. A Christian marriage is a 1 + 1 = 3 equation between a male and female united to glorify Christ. An unknown author writes this poem titled *Marriage Still Takes Three* and is excellent advice for those who are about to get married.

> I once thought marriage took
>
> Just two to make a go,
>
> But now I am convinced
>
> It takes the Lord also.
>
> And not one marriage fails
>
> Where Christ is asked to enter,
>
> As lovers come together
>
> With Jesus at the center.
>
> But marriage seldom thrives,

And homes are incomplete,

He is welcomed there

To help avoid defeat.

In homes where Christ is first,

It's obvious to see,

Those unions work,

For marriage still takes three.

Man struggles for a sense of worth, purpose, and distinctiveness based on conditions he attempts to achieve and maintains outside of God's values. Millions of people reject God at an early age because of experiencing unattractive lives. Some people are going to hear what they want to hear and thereby justify their sinful acts against God.

The causes of stress and breakdown in marriage are many and complex. Rapid social change always brings some weakening of traditional values and religious convictions.

Marriages today face a manifold of problems. Covenant marriage has sailed into troubled waters. Economic and social conditions, abuse of alcohol, and a lack of communication between the partners create stresses for marriage. Infidelity has blown away the happiness of marriage. These influences have shaped attitudes against life-long marriage. The increase of industrialization and the movement of families away from rural areas into cities have generated a separation from grandparents who in the past had an essential role in handing on the faith and moral values to their grandchildren. These values have become destabilized in every sphere of life, spiritually and politically.

On the horizon are some warnings. The first warning has to do with the overly aggressive nature of society. The second warning is the counterproductive results of being fruitful and multiplying. The third warning of marriage is a concept to replace the old plan with contemporary models. Therefore, we burden ourselves with making decisions God has already made. We do what we want to do, do what we feel like doing, and not be obligated to do God's will. Society is in trouble when we sit, taking life easy, and make rules to keep humanity rationality in a perspective that shows little respect for God.

The reasonability of marriage has sailed into deep waters. It should continue to be a process by which a male and female make a proposal public, making a covenant until death do, them apart, but increasingly is cut short by intolerance. Of course, over time personalities change, bodies age, and the romantic love waxes and wanes. These should not be excuses to change the beauty of covenant marriage. No marriage is free of conflict, and the couple who learns how to handle confrontation peacefully will survive. A marriage that is going to survive and manage the problems that inevitably arise must stay focused on Jesus. If Jesus is in the union, who can ever be against it?

Humanity is in the business of playing with marriage. Marriages are not a game. It is the oldest ordinance of God in continual effect. It must be done as God has put it together, let no man come up with a different plan. It will become deadly and will destroy covenant marriage. He is the inventor of marriage.

Contrary to the Western culture of "falling in love" as a prerequisite to marriage, there is another quality of marriage that must be decided upon by Christians before they are ready to ask God to join the two to become one flesh.

Married life is real. Covenant marriage is in a suicidal traffic jam as some view the general atmosphere of surliness and hostility. I remember hearing that men were once shoppers looking for the right mate to buy like a holiday Barbie doll! Are we ready for the depression, the anxiety, and rage that accompanies a secular expedition? Contemporary marriage is a fantasy of the secular world. Even for those who manage to have some wishes fulfilled, the season will be over quickly, before the decorations come down. Secularism deprives the spiritual celebration of male and female in covenant marriage. Paul warns us, "Casting down imaginations, and every high thing that exalt itself against the knowledge of God and bringing into captivity every thought to the obedience of Christ" (2 Cor. 10:5). We can easily find ourselves preparing to sing "O Holy Night" or living in an unholy nightmare. For many who faithfully want to engage in secular marriage it is a necessary prelude to disappointment.

God created humanity in his image, in the image of God created them; male and female, He created them. God blessed them and said to them, "And God blessed them, and God said unto them, be fruitful, and multiply, and replenish the earth, and subdue it" (Gen. 1:28). In the last fifty years, same-sex marriages, marriage to animals and things, were considered abnormal behavior and offered no possible resolution to being fruitful and creating humankind. The only thing that's multiplying is the numbers of males and females engaging in same-sex marriages. No longer is same-sex marriage and other types classified as abnormal. Today, marriage has developed an "anything goes" atmosphere. It was only a matter of time before other lifestyles would become accepted.

People practicing same sex-marriage are not considered criminals by society; it is fully embraced by much of the gay community. The Western world today has merited popularity demands that have not reinforced the messages of covenant marriage. A spiritual sickness occurs when we exclude identity with God. Some traditional ideas remain, but with a different cast. The uncertainty and corruption in marriage has been brought about by a political transition, globalization, and individualism to the extent that the vision for covenant marriage has suffered.

The dilemma is that some deep levels of distress have developed in society. The unchristian are on a mission to destroy the Christian view of covenant marriage. Whether we are wise or foolish, male or female, we should care for the things that please God. But society is engaged in the presumption that it is all right to leave these presupposition norms with a message that does not transform the hearers. The fundamental structures of old ideas are disappearing. The spiritual concerns don't remain to stand, and religious convictions remain in isolation or compartmentalization, and it does not defend covenant marriage at large.

A dramatic decrease in covenant marriage has developed in the United States and around the world. The problem is a response to contemporary issues of same-sex marriage, and marriage to animals or things have invaded the paradigm. The enculturation of modern scientific developments has influenced and structured covenant marriage in such a way that it has lost its mission identity and moral character and concerns for future generations.

Today we live in an age in which commitment within marriage has become rare. When I married, it had strict rules of conduct. Giovanna Boldrini offers some standard of conduct in 1950 compared to 2019:

1. A wife was never supposed to challenge or question her husband. No way this would fly nowadays!

2. The wives were told to wear pink underwear, but they were supposed to be lacy and frilly ones. Today women are stylish.

3. Except when Dad is around, it was the wife's job to keep the kids well-behaved. Women today know that parenting is a shared responsibility.

4. Cooking was done by the female to keep the man loyal. Today, we have stay-at-home dads.

5. A wife's sexuality was a delicate balancing act. Today's women are free to express themselves however they choose.

6. Wives were to remember that the man is in charge. Today, in many places, women are running the show.

God's plan is for one woman and one man to commit to each other exclusively and permanently. It takes some spiritual discipline requiring time, work, determination, and a commitment that builds faith and develops character in the relationship.

A significant shift in sexual attitudes toward marriage has promoted alternative lifestyles, with mass media constantly depicting relationships without commitment as fun and faithfulness as monotonous. The tragic result is an explosion of terrible consequences: broken homes, abandoned children, depression, crime, substance abuse, and sexually transmitted diseases that remain with us today.

In the Old and New Testaments, the Bible condemns sexual acts between members of the same sex or animals. "Thou shalt not lie with mankind, as with womankind: it is abomination" (Lev. 18:22). The Lord requires of his people, "There shall be no whore of the daughters of Israel, nor a sodomite of the sons of Israel. Thou shalt not bring the hire of a whore, or the price of a dog, into the house of the LORD thy God for any vow: for even both these are abomination unto the LORD thy God" (Deut. 23:17–18). Such abomination was forbidden in Israel and should be in our society. Leviticus 20:13 says, "If a man also lies with mankind, as he lieth with a woman, both of them have committed an abomination: they shall surely be put to death; their blood shall be upon them" (Lev. 20:13).

God designed the union of marriage to stabilize sexual intimacy and protection of male, female, parent-and-child relationships in a covenant marriage. Its purpose and design serve as a pattern or model of the relationship God wants you to have in a covenant marriage.

Douglas Farrow's tells us that marriage is an institution that orders persons to the common good, arising from the natural differences of male and female, the complementarity of which is crucial for the fulfillment of the individual's good. Sexual difference, he claims, and not inclination or desire, is foundational for the "existence and well-being of the human race." Sexual differences in marriage style have certainly changed to same-sex marriages, marriage to animals and things like cars.

What has happened to marriage in America and around the world is quite alarming. LifeWay researchers solicited 2,000 people's responses on issues facing today's family in America. Paul Stevens says, "Marriage has surrendered to culture and need to reestablish a biblical view. We must put God back in his rightful place and choose to live up to the standards of covenant marriage and family." People's lack of grounding in biblical teaching on marriage and the family is the cause of many problems. Here are some results:

1. Anti-Christian culture

2. Divorce

3. Busyness

4. Absent father figure

5. Lack of discipline

6. Financial pressures

7. Lack of communication

8. Negative media influences

9. Balance of work and family

10. Materialism

How did we get here? Dr. Fred Lowery, author of the book *Covenant Marriage*, says:

- People are marrying less and cohabitating more.

- Waiting longer to get married has become the trend.

- The divorce rate has skyrocketed.

- Families have children.

- Births have dramatically increased out of wedlock.

- Both parents are working outside the home.

- Same-sex marriages are widely accepted.

- In America, the standards of a covenant marriage have disappeared and are fading into the distant past.

CHAPTER FOUR

Compatibility of Man and Woman

God created humanity in His image at the beginning of creation. "So, God created man in his own image, in the image of God created he him; male and female created he them" (Gen. 1:27). "There is neither Jew nor Greek, there is neither bond nor free, there is neither male nor female: for ye are all one in Christ Jesus" (Gal. 3:28). God has an intended purpose for what man and a woman should be. And every part of our identities will be affected by how we live out that design. A man and a woman are different psychologically. An attempt to change them would violate creation design and purpose. Our differences are the little pinches of salt, which can make us seem sweeter. We communicate differently. We smile differently and brush our hair differently.

The union of marriage is patterned after Christ and the Church. Paul says, "This is a great mystery: but I speak concerning Christ and the church" (Eph. 5:32). Becoming one is a portrayal of a covenant between man and a woman and between Christ and his church. A disruption of the marital design defaces the icon of the gospel of Jesus Christ.

If you find yourself called to embrace the dignity and fixed meaning of your purpose, "So God created man in his own image, in the image of God created he him; male and female created he them" (Gen.1:27). God has put you here because He is out to achieve something in the gender, He wrapped you in.

A male becomes the husband, and a female becomes the wife. Then the relationship establishes a father and mother to formulate an alliance called the family. There are five things that tie the relationship of woman to the man.

1. A woman is man's helper.

2. The rib.

3. When Adam named her Eve.

4. The full aspect of the relationship is cleaved together. It means the husband is to stick to his wife.

5. They both were naked and unashamed.

God created man to be a leader in the marriage and the family relationship. A woman was designed to help man accomplish his God-given tasks. Man is called to be the leader, and the woman is called to be the helper; she is not to be a slave to man.

A hammer and a screwdriver are different tools designed for different jobs. A man and woman are different by design and have a fixed purpose. Humanity can't create a definition of manhood and womanhood.

God made neither superior over the other, but they are distinct, like Beauty and the Beast. God made a man stronger because he was to be the provider and the protector of the family. He is divinely fitted for masculine success. Durable, intelligent, and favored by God. He was made to have more energy, given the strength to protect the woman, and muscles for digging and working. A male and a female are different in some respect. A male is more a rational creature; a female is more of an emotional being. There are more distinctions between the male and female, but all of you are one in Christ Jesus. We need to do better at fulfilling our role. An attempt to change these differences or desires violates God's basic design.

The first reason God made a woman is for man's companionship. The second reason is for cooperation. The third reason is God made a woman for man's completion. God created Eve for Adam's companionship, meaning she was perfect for the plan and design. He did not make anything else to match a man and a woman because they are created in His image. Eve is God's design suited to God's purpose. She is to be the one to share man's responsibilities, respond to his nature with understanding and love, and to cooperate with him in working out the plan of God.

When you cherish one another, you must recognize that you are made in God's image and are, therefore, of infinite worth and value. A healthy marriage is cherished by nourishing togetherness, expressing a covenant of love and strength, encouraging one another daily. You have made a lifelong commitment, a full and earnest investment of your whole self as the most valuable treasure of a lifetime.

When we consider choosing a godly mate, there are many qualities of a man or woman; this is where the marriage gets off course. We come into a marriage with too many attributes and expectations he or she is seeking.

A male is more aggressive, emotionally stable, controllable, more irritable, excitable, inpatient, boastful, businesslike, nomadic, greater depth of maturity, direct, truthful, sportsmanlike, democratic, hunter, fighter, provider, defender, and more caring.

A wise husband relies on the Holy Spirit and not upon one's abilities. Husbands who seek to be great servants are faithful, available, and teachable. "Husbands love your wives, even as Christ also loved the church, and gave himself for it" (Eph. 5:25). Paul devotes twice as many words to telling husbands to love their wives as to telling wives to submit to their husbands. How should a man love his wife? (1) He should be willing to sacrifice everything for her. (2) He should make her well-being of primary importance. "Let love and faithfulness never leave you" (Prov. 3:3). "So, ought men to love their wives as their own bodies. He that loveth his wife loveth himself" (Eph. 5:28). "Wives submit yourselves unto your own husbands, as unto the Lord" (Eph. 5:22).

A husband is to love her, respect her, provide for her, comfort her, honor and cherish her, in sickness and in health, in prosperity and in adversity, and forsaking all other and keep himself for her alone long as he shall live." A loving husband assumes the role of leadership and the burden of providing the needs of the family. He must not become toughminded or bitter, because this is not what God intended. The wife helps in many ways, but she does not do his job for him. A husband who is living a life of ease, not taking care of his responsibilities…that marriage will soon fall apart. "But if any provide not for his own, and especially for those of his own house, he hath denied the faith, and is worse than an infidel" (1 Tim. 5:8). The wife is a helper to her partner, but she is not obligated to do his share of the work. There is no excuse for laziness by any husband to delegate his work to the spouse and live a comfortable life.

We continuously look at Proverbs 31 to reveal the qualities of an ideal woman. Most women will ask the question, "What are the qualities of an ideal husband?"

1. A wise husband is kind, humble, compassionate, honest, and a good breadwinner for his family.

2. A wise husband is truthful and exercises self-control.

3. A wise husband has a gentle tongue, and he is generous.

4. A wise husband is a good listener and is willing to be corrected (even by his wife). He has complete confidence in his wife's faithfulness and trust.

5. A wise husband is not contentious, but a peacemaker.

6. A thoughtful husband has control of his temper and avoids excesses. He expresses his faith in his wife's abilities by giving her the freedom to function without unnecessary hindrances.

7. A wise husband has a concern for others.

8. A wise husband has self-confidence, and his family is proud of him.

9. A wise husband fears God and is obedient to His Word.

10. A wise husband is not a jealous man and loves his wife and children. He appreciates the value of his wife but gives her the praise she deserves.

Men are sometimes strange beings. Women are fidgety. Men, as they grow older, forget to remember their marriage vows and make excuses for not continuing the journey. They don't calculate their behavior as warranted, but acceptable. A common problem in young marriages is when the husband or wife has their feelings hurt by their spouse. They tell Mommy, Daddy, or friends how hurt they are. When they feel better, they go back and make up with their spouse. Mommy and Daddy grow to hate their daughter or son-in-law.

Marriage is like wine; it ought to get better as its ages. But for some, it gets worst because of the appetite of some spouse changes. Some old coon wants a mate as young as a baby kitten. The wife refuses to be a remote control, and the husband wants to abandon her because of a lack of his power over her.

Some extensive research has concluded some twenty-first century standards for measuring a man. The results are quite impressive.

1. His ability to make and conserve money.

2. The car cost, style, and age.

3. How much hair on his head?

4. Strength and size.

5. How much success on the job?

6. What sports played or enjoyed.

7. How many club memberships he joins?

8. Aggressiveness and reliability.

A female is more submissive, the hunter for things, fighter, provider, dependent, helper, made to be loved, sensitive, and a male's greatest asset. A man is insufficient and needs a partner. But they are both created with equal status in God's image. Genesis 1:27 tell us, "God created man in his image, in the image of God he created him; male and female he created them." They are distinctively male and female, created for different complementary roles.

God values a woman who is submissive. It is a sign of strength that a woman is submitting herself to God and is obeying His commands. A woman who cannot stand between God and her family will repeat the error of Eve. A woman who submits to her husband and God understands authority and leadership. When a woman submits to her husband's authority in marriage, she is beautiful to God. "Submissive" is not a popular word in our society today. Many people think being submissive is weak. God requires the wife to be submissive to her husband.

A godly woman should not have an argumentative, quarrelsome, or belligerent personality that is contentious, combative, antagonistic spirit, quick to anger, and very selfish. She should be a lady that is peace-loving to others and respectful to her husband. It is excellent to live with this woman.

God has established the role of a woman in the home. The role of the wife greatly enhances the leadership of her husband, but she does not lead her husband. The leadership of the wife is having authority in the home. Women, in the Old Testament, were not priests, nor were they given command over men in public worship. While we must be quick to stress the freedoms given the godly woman, we must also be honest about those areas reserved for men only, not because women were incapable of leading, but because of divine principles governing the roles of men and women in spiritual leadership.

St. Thomas Aquinas tells us, "We must look at a woman in two ways: in herself (as a spiritual being, made for man) and to man (as a biological entity created for man, in a way that man is created for her, reproduction and in union).

The role of women has changed in many countries, and they have gained positions in public life equal to that of men. A new range of possibilities once restricted is opening for them, and they are getting further away from the home and the will of God.

Our society is obsessed with beauty! But is there more to beauty than what meets the eye? We live in a society that places a high degree of importance on physical appearance. Television, movies, magazines, and billboards all display attractive women. We see men and women engaged in plastic surgery to enhance their appearance. If there is any beauty found in a woman, it is striving to be more like Jesus.

A woman's body has been fashioned to be beautiful. God designed her to be that way. Her hair, skin is soft, appealing, and her body is fashioned to attract men. However, the physical features are a small part of what makes a woman truly beautiful. God did not make a man to be attractive to another man, or a woman to be attractive to another woman, or animals and things. Our society has placed a high emphasis on the physical aspect of beauty outside the spiritual realm.

The LORD says, "Moreover the LORD saith, Because the daughters of Zion are haughty, and walk with stretched forth necks and wanton eyes, walking and mincing as they go, and making a tinkling with their feet. Therefore, the Lord will smite with a scab the crown of the head of the daughters of Zion, and the LORD will discover their secret parts. In that day the Lord will take away the bravery of their tinkling ornaments about their feet, and their cauls and their round tires like the moon. The chains, and the bracelets, and the mufflers. The bonnets, and the ornaments of the legs, and the headbands, and the tablets, and the earrings. The rings, and nose jewels. The changeable suits of apparel, and the mantles, and the wimples, and the crisping pins. The glasses, and the fine linen, and the hoods, and the vails. And it shall come to pass, that instead of sweet smell there shall be stink; and instead of a girdle a rent; and instead of well-set hair baldness; and instead of a stomacher a girding of sackcloth; and burning instead of beauty" (Isa. 3:16–24).

A woman ought to dress beautifully, but not like a harlot. There are some things that women should not wear outside the home. Today, some women wear fashions a silkworm could weave during his coffee break. Proverbs 7:10 says, "

And, behold, there met him a woman with the attire of a harlot, and subtill of heart." Some women say, I am trying to be attractive; then you need to ask yourself what are trying to attract.

Some fashions you wear only your husband should see. Proverbs 11 says, "She is loud and stubborn; her feet abide not in her house" (Prov. 11:12). A woman should not be loud and stubborn, especially in public.

A truly gorgeous woman is physically and spiritually appealing. Women tend to look at their features, and men tend to look at the overall impression a woman creates. Physical beauty is within reach of any woman. God was angry with the women of Israel with their outward appearance. When a person is all about their outward appearance, their skin, hair, and clothes, they are people seeking to glorify themselves instead of trying to glorify God. Because of this pride, God judged the women of Israel.

I admire my wife for her physical beauty, but I am attracted to her inner qualities. She is a woman, kind and gracious. Proverbs 11:16 tells us that a polite woman retains honor, is virtuous, kind, gentle, thoughtful, and unselfish. In Proverbs 31:26, a virtuous woman is described as having the law of kindness on her tongue. I love kind women. Men are suckers for kindness and consideration. We love women who are sociable, flexible, easygoing. Most men cannot resist a sweet woman. Women who are gracious and kind are attractive.

A woman should also have good judgment. If a woman lacks discretion, it takes away from her beauty and value. Good judgment is needed in carrying out the duties of a godly woman, such as moral issues, money matters, choices, decisions, dealing with others, taking care of the family, and work. A woman who possesses good judgment is of great value because she can be trusted to do the right thing. "A gracious woman retain honor" (Prov. 11:22).

A woman should continue to grow and become better spiritually. Proverbs 31 describes a woman who is competent and capable of developing her talents and abilities. She contributes these abilities to be used by her family, church, community, and others. A woman who is developing her potential is an attractive woman.

Some marriages in the Bible seem less than ideal, but they had God on their side. Sarah and Abraham had their problems. Sarah was cranky and bossy. Job's wife was inconsistent during his trials. In a covenant marriage, the wife submits to her husband to transform him. "Likewise, ye wives, be in subjection to your own husbands; that, if any obey not the word, they also may without the word be won by the conversation of the wives" (1 Pet. 3:1).

Very few people have read Proverbs 31 considering what it teaches husbands about wives in ancient times. They would never have this kind of freedom, responsibility, support, and encouragement in contemporary times. The character of the godly woman is not a model we share today. The standards for an ideal wife in Western culture is different in every marriage. There will be extremes in some relationships that throw all "rules" out the window. If most men are ideal husbands and appreciate their wives, they will have no excuses not to conform.

Proverbs 31 summarizes an ideal wife in our culture today as one diligent and kind. She works with her hands out in the world. She rises early in the morning and retires late from working in management, business, financial operations, occupations, advertising, promotions manager, biomedical engineer, education administrator, human resources manager, and others. The salaries start at $46,000 to $95,000 annually. The ideal wife will not sit around the house all day watching soap operas, home decorating shows, cooking shows, television sitcoms, for she has no idle time. The ideal wife speaks with wisdom beyond practical wisdom, for she can make a wise decision about investments. I have been happy married to my wife, and if I had to do it again, I would marry the same woman!

The argument does not command the husband to take over responsibilities, nor does it commend the woman who would do so contrary to her husband's will. I urge the husband to give his wife more freedom, but it does not teach the wives to take advantage of what is given. But the freedom is often attributed to her, and value as a wife to him.

Let's draw your attention to the kind of man this "ideal husband" had to be for his ideal wife to be what she was described to be. How does the wife complement and help the husband in his responsibilities? The Hebrew word for *wife* is gender-specific; it cannot mean anything other than "a woman." The ideal wife today is restricted largely to dirty dishes and diapers, doing the housework, and taking care of the children alone. Proverbs 31 widens the horizon of what a godly wife and mother ought to be, encouraged by the perfect husband.

A woman is to be man's lawful wedded wife, to live together according to God's commandments. She is to assume the responsibilities of headship over the home. A woman is to love her husband, respect him, provide for him, comfort him, honor and cherish him, in sickness and in health, in prosperity and in adversity, and forsaking all other and keep herself for him long as they both shall live.

The husband must come to grips with some radical changes in thinking his wife is not a slave. The husband is expected to fulfill his role in the marriage, fully utilizing his gifts and abilities. The husband should not threaten his wife's competence. He is frightened by the thought that his wife can do some things better than he can, so he carefully fences off these areas, even though his wife desires to serve him in his role.

God has commanded wives to submit themselves to their husband's authority. It does not mean that a woman should never have an opinion to say what takes place in the family. A wise husband will consult his wife on all critical issues.

The purpose of marriage is complete. God created Eve, and Adam must make marriage to achieve God's purpose. The purpose is not a reflection of a relationship between other creatures or things. The connection is between him and her, a male and female.

When men look for a wonderful woman, the attraction is viewed from how she looks on the outside. I was attracted to my wife; whose personality was excellent on the inside. The measuring stick for me was my mother. I look for a spouse whose quality was very much like my mother's and not because of beauty. It was the beauty that sparks from the inside of her that impressed me when she stood as my spouse. Being beautiful on the inside makes you attractive on the outside, and this should be the top priority on every man's list when he looks for a mate. The Apostle Peter states, "Do not let your adornment be merely outward looking at arranging the hair, wearing gold, or putting on fine apparel. Let it be the hidden person of the heart, with the incorruptible beauty of a gentle and quiet spirit, which is very precious in the sight of God" (1 Pet. 3:3–4).

Ngina Otiende, certified marriage coach and author, suggests five ways to love your husband through every marriage season.

1. Fall in love with prayer. Pray often for him; it's your weapon against fear and worry and everything that will try to steal his heart and mind.

2. Understand how your husband processes things differently because he is a man.

3. Get over self and remove some expectations. Let go of some of your rights and expectations.

4. Take care of yourself. Cultivate your interests.

5. Walk through the seasons expecting help. Get out of your comfort zone when you need help.

Michael Kercheval suggests six ways to love your wife:

1. Show her daily you love her. Shower her with accolades that are lovely.

2. Acknowledge the work your spouse does in the home, or out of the house.

3. Your spouse is a diligent woman riding in and taking over some of the family duties during stressful times.

4. Keep an open hand to communication.

5. Set goals together.

6. Remember, keeping the romance in your relationship is key to showing your wife that you love her.

There are confident attitudes existing among women's roots in the feminist movement and is still prevalent among individual segments of society. This attitude is a deep anger toward men. Some women want to prove that they are just as good as their male counterparts and that they don't need them.

Eve got caught up in the serpent's words, and it all sounded too good to pass up. Eve believed the offer was more than God had given. She found more pain, sorrow, and shame. When she sinned, God blamed Adam. Adam tried to blame God but when Eve sinned, God blamed Adam. "And the eyes of them both were opened, and they knew that they were naked; and they sewed fig leaves together and made themselves aprons" (Gen. 3:7). God had given clear instructions to Adam to take care of the garden and not to eat from the tree of knowledge. God removed them from the garden and cursed them.

"Unto the woman he said, I will greatly multiply thy sorrow and thy conception; in sorrow thou shalt bring forth children; and thy desire shall be to thy husband, and he shall rule over thee" (Gen. 3:16). God said to Adam, "Because thou hast hearkened unto the voice of thy wife, and hast eaten of the tree, of which I commanded thee, saying, thou shalt not eat of it: cursed is the ground for thy sake; in sorrow shalt thou eat of it all the days of thy life. Thorns also and thistles shall it bring forth to thee; and thou shalt eat the herb of the field. In the sweat of thy face shalt thou eat bread, till thou return unto the ground; for out of it was thou taken for dust thou art, and unto dust shalt thou return" (Gen. 3:17–19).

Covenant marriage strives to serve God, and the couple learns in the process, as a wife and a husband. A marriage that does not glorify God will have setbacks. When individuals look for a mate, the right chemistry is between a male and a female.

Today, the damaging attitude about marriage is going to cause God's wrath to come against humanity once again. You can now say, I am going to do it God's way. God will bless your marriage because I believe He will keep His promises.

My grace is enough for you (2 Cor. 12:9).

Trust in the Lord with all your heart, and do not lean on your understanding. In all your ways acknowledge Him, and He will make your paths straight (Prov. 3:5–6).

For I know the plans that I have for you, declares the Lord, plans for welfare and not for calamity to give you a future and a hope (Jer. 29:11).

I can do all things through Christ who strengthens me (Phil. 4:13).

The husband and wife need to love each other as if it depends on every breath taken. There is a principle about love in action here.

Love covers. Paul is defining love when he writes that love "Bear all things, believeth all things, hope all things, endure all things" (1 Cor. 13:7). Love is an inward expression of an outward emotion. Don't tell me how much you love me; show me what you mean with words and actions. Christ loved the Church and gave Himself up for her that He might sanctify her, having cleansed her by the washing of water with the word, that He might present to Himself the Church in all her glory, having no spot or wrinkle or any such thing; but that she should be holy and blameless.

Husband and wife are made in the image of God compatible for each other. We are made a little different to serve each other for the purpose we were made and created. Love is the cement that holds it all together. To my wife - Carolyn Ruffin:

It is the love I have for thee.

I have seen everything you do.

And after all these years, your beauty still inspires me

In everything you do.

I love because of you

It Is the love I have for thee

All the things you have sacrificed.

And the moments you had shared with me.

Your love is worth all the best that I will ever have of

value.

Love that unconditional.

Love that everlasting

It Is the love I have for thee

I gaze upon your face

You are all that can be.

Until death, do us apart.

Then loving you are meant to be.

I love thee more each day

It Is the love I have for thee

CHAPTER FIVE

Fighting In Marriage

Most fights in marriages start from a little spark, and soon it becomes a fire. Forest fires often start from small sparks that bloom into massive, intense fires. You are going to have fights, and they can also be the kind of fight whereby no physical contact occurs. What causes fights and quarrels among you?

Most couples fight because of marital unhappiness. They often say, "We fell out of love, we've grown apart, or we fight too much." Such issues can be remedied if both partners want to do so.

All marriages have problems. Couples get into heated discussions. Some couples behave as if they were married by the Secretary of War and every issue is resolved by the Justice of the Peace. James's formula for handling marital confrontations is, "Wherefore, my beloved brethren, let every man be swift to hear, slow to speak, slow to wrath" (Jas. 1:19).

Announcing itself with 145-mph winds, on August 29, 2005, Hurricane Katrina slammed into the Gulf Coast just outside New Orleans on Monday, submerging entire neighborhoods up to their roofs, swamping beachfronts, blowing out windows in hospitals, hotels, and high-rises. Fighting can slam a marriage like a hurricane with destructive forces. Your destructive behavior in a marriage can blow everything out of balance. Some marriages become disestablished when the couples are not able to manage challenges, such as challenges of resolving their conflict, sexual fulfillment, good communication, mutual commitment, childbearing and rearing.

Have you had someone come to you and say, "I've been watching you, and there is something different about you"? They wanted whatever it was that you have. Many lives are changed because of your commitment to God in your marriage. Is there anything in your life right now that can point to immorality, or is just plain wrong?

Covenant marriage starts with the fragrance of ever-lasting love but ends a long way from death do us part. We live in the days of abounding iniquity and dwindling love. People in this world need the ability to love and to be loved more than anything else. Marriages are sick, and what they need now is love, love, love. A kind of love that makes the trip worthwhile. We need to love one another, and there is a great need for just old-fashioned love in marriage. I never witnessed my grandmother and grandfather fighting. They were a different breed than Mom and Dad.

There are three reasons why fighting happens in marriages. We fight because of envy and jealousy, because of desires and wants, and because of a lack of trust in the relationship. When we get married, we come into the union with childish ways and spoiled appetites. Paul says, "When I was a child, I spoke as a child, I understood as a child, I thought as a child: but when I became a man, I put away childish things." (1 Cor. 13:11).

The marriage should be thicker than mud and as strong as steel. The oneness is joined, as one blood you stand; divided, you fall. God is the witness that you are obligated to one another by doing good deeds. You must live to be faithful as a husband and wife. In

God, you put all your trust and encourage each other to fulfill your dreams, refusing to let anything tear you apart.

Each day you must love and not despise. In times of sorrow, you must remain united and endure hard times without fighting. According to D. R. Mace, author of the book *Close companions: The marriage enrichment handbook,* tells us marriage requires three things: (1) a high degree of motivation, (2) a desire to make the marriage work, and (3) a willingness to expend personal time and effort to make sure it does. Fighting directs one toward self-justification and redirecting oneself toward self-examination and self-gratification. It's about individual personal desires. People are tempted when they are enticed by their own evil desires (Jas. 4:1–2).

We become territorial like wild animals and do whatever possible to call attention to, protect, or defend our rights and desires in marriage. The Apostle James contends, "Ye lust, and have not: ye kill, and desire to have, and cannot obtain: ye fight and war, yet ye have not, because ye ask not (Jas. 4:2). Desire wage war against your soul, and you fight to control the relationship. If I am not in control of them, I want out of this situation immediately. The married couple will agree that it is wrong for men to exploit the vulnerability of women that provokes fear. Women should not use their verbal strength to bully men to shaming.

Jo Robinson, the author of *Hot Monogamy,* interviewed fifteen hundred couples regarding relationships; some critical data came from the research.

1. Women can see how men can be physically abusive, but they do not see their power to invoke shame on their spouse.

2. Women don't understand how men want to please them. Men live to please them.

3. Women interpret withdrawal as uncaring, resulting in criticism and unhappiness.

Most fights are in a quest for control to monitor the money in the family and making all decisions that affect the marriage, where we go on vacation and turning the light off at night. Your spouse goes on and on until she thinks, "I am being treated like a child." If you take all the rights from a child, they will soon learn to be rebellious. A husband who treats their mate this way...that marriage will lead to self-destruction.

James says, "Ye lust, and have not: ye kill, and desire to have, and cannot obtain: ye fight and war (Jas. 4:2). Fights occur when you justify your role by rationalizing and justifying the actions of war already in your heart. The desire for things to satisfy your pleasures, like power and possessions, makes you fight for them. It is because of selfishness.

Webster's describes selfishness as the quality or state of being selfish; regard to one's interest or happiness; that leads a person to direct his purposes to the advancement of his excitement, power, or joy, without regarding for others. "For none of us lives for ourselves alone, and none of us dies for ourselves alone" (Rom. 14:7).

Another translation of selfishness may suggest that "I want," even if it signifies gaining evil desires through lust. James says it will become a passion. You want, and you do not have. You murder and covet, quarrel and fight, and you do not have because you do not ask. You ask, and you do not receive because you ask wickedly (Jas. 4:1–3). It is a tragedy that an individual passion can cripple the marriage externally and internally. You need to seek some measure of healing and purification through counseling.

Why do we fight in marriages? Fights occur because we desire something, and we are not able to get it peacefully. We need to stop fighting and begin loving our mate rather than what we covet. Humility sees one's faults, in contrast to insincerity or dishonesty.

Every fight in marriage is a rebellious act against something. It seems as if it is not a war against oneself, but it is a war within oneself. The root cause of every fight, external or internal, is rebellion against God! What God has put together, let no one set apart. God is not the author of envy and jealousy. When we fraternize with the enemy and allow him into our marriage, peace becomes distorted and destroys the marriage. How often do you argue with your partner? Howard J. Markman, Scott M. Stanley, Susan L. Blumberg, authors of the book *Fighting for Your Marriage*, suggest that couples watch for danger signs that escalate into fighting.

1. Don't let little arguments escalate into ugly fights with accusations, criticisms, name-calling, or bringing up past hurts.

2. Don't criticize or belittle your spouse's opinions, feelings, or desires.

3. Don't view your spouse's words or actions more negatively than they are meant to be.

4. When you have a problem to solve, don't act like you are on opposite teams.

5. Sometimes it is better to hold back from telling your spouse what you really think and feel.

6. Don't isolate self in the relationship when issues occur. Work out a solution quickly.

7. When you argue, don't withdraw. One of you must become a peacemaker.

When the institution of marriage is torn apart with practical idealism, human society becomes contrary to the plan of God for marriage. Any thought, conduct, belief, which becomes anti-God or anti-Christ will open the door for other ingredients to enter and become inhumanly inconsistent with God and Christ. The lawful humanist desires of marriage will lead you away from God. These desires wage war with God and within you and fight against the Spirit of God. Marriage becomes a work of the flesh, forming a relationship with the concurring objective of an institution directly in conflict with God. More and more fights will occur in marriages because the value system, the principles that hold your marriage together, are altered, redirected, and remodeled.

Every marriage has a foundation; without one, it could not be stable or stay standing for long. It will have to stand against storms, earthquakes, and weather. The better the foundation, the more durable the marriage; the same is real in life. If we establish a foundation based on a relationship with God in the marriage, we will easily endure the storms of matrimony with fewer nights at the fights.

Marriage requires a healthy relationship. Secondly, it is the relationship with the covenant of marriage. Thirdly, a relationship with God. In the realm of personal relationships, however, all three operate together, and they set the standard by which a person is judged. Sometimes you can tell what a man wants by listening to what he complains about. It is all good until you put a man and a woman together. If you and your spouse are repeatedly having conflicts that become hostile, there is a chance that you may start to feel some hopelessness about your ability to resolve disagreements as a team to keep marriage happy. Conflicts can start when one spouse continuously imposes a Burger King philosophy, "I want to have it my way or no way." If this kind of behavior sticks around, it will lead to depression for your spouse.

Another problem in marriage is violence. "A soft answer turns away wrath: but grievous words stir up anger" (Prov. 15:1). "Be not hasty in thy spirit to be angry: for anger rest in the bosom of fools." (Eccles. 7:9). Violence in a marriage relationship will create immediate and long-lasting damage. It is difficult to trust or communicate with a person who responds in anger most of the time; it will break down the relationship.

Violence will kill a relationship. It comes from the difficulty of controlling one's behavior trigger by desires to lash out at your spouse because you are upset over issues that build up over time. Anger can lead to fighting, high blood pressure, and eventually, physical abuse. Communicating with someone who lashes out is difficult.

Some marriages continue to fall apart because one mate has all the desires and neglects the wishes of the other and sets all the goals for himself. Often, most spouses will admit, there is nothing wrong with me, so I don't need to change. Protecting your relationship means keeping issues and conflicts from wrecking or intruding on the great times that bonded you together.

You can change your partner by changing you. If I am doing something and it affects my spouse's behavior and it leads to adverse reactions, then I need to look at the cause of the action and change. For example, I know a couple who had problems with finances. One spouse was always buying the automobile of his choice, but rarely letting his partner choose what she likes. It led to a breakdown in the relationship because the behavior continued when they made other significant decisions.

You are joined together in a partnership. Let me show you how it works. There are some things we must accept from each other. People are different because of their personality. You may like the color of the car when I'm concerned with the model. Husbands and wives are different because of their character.

You want because of what you like but are willing to take what comes with the model. Some husbands rationalize their mate as dumb, stupid, and ignorant because the spouse refuses to cooperate as he requires. He becomes a master of outrageous behavior because his spouse spends funds on her respective family. Therefore, the husband begins to complain about how the wife spends her money. But the wife goes to work each day just as he does and makes a significant contribution to the family bank account. He spent his funds on tennis equipment and technological innovations. He likes to buy fancy items for himself like expensive clothing, tools, automobiles, and travel.

The husband begins to flex his muscles; I am the husband, you are the wife, and you should submit to me. The wife is a brilliant woman who wants to defend her integrity. She is a fair lady. She loves to cook and invites her family over on Sunday for dinner or when the husband is out of town. She loves to buy things for her family, but the husband is complaining that she should use her money to help him with their finances. He leaves the wife at home when he travels. They fight over these issues. He needs to compromise so that each can get something in return.

Marriage problems can be solved: talk it out, make the adjustments, make accommodations that make the house a peaceful home, and accept the outcome. Don't let Dad, Mom, sister, brother, in-laws, friends, buddies, help you make up your mind. You are not married to your mom, dad, sister, brother, or friends. You are married to your wife; one whom you have selected as the most beautiful woman in the world. You are ready to love and cherish her for the rest of your life. Make her believe that there is no mistake about the choice.

Patricia Love and Steven Stosny, authors of the book *How to improve your marriage without talking about it*, offers a list of things that trigger anger in marriage.

- Words hurt and destroy and can trigger anger.
- Excluding each other from important decisions.
- You are robbing each of the opportunity to help by overdoing.
- I was questioning what one said and one's judgment.
- You are implying inadequacy.
- You are ignoring one's advice.
- He is making unrealistic demands of time and energy.
- You are criticizing your spouse's choices and behavior.
- Focusing on what I didn't get, not what I did.
- You are withholding praise.
- Using a harsh tone. Valuing others' needs over your spouse's needs.
- Name-calling and belittling and criticizing his/her family.
- We are making irrational statements at the wrong time.

Divorce, a last-ditch option, has become a major vacation destination from the realities of marriage. The most devastating problem in a marriage is divorce. It is like a destructive storm in any marriage. It is stressful, discouraging, and damaging. It tears up homes, families. Children are reared by grandparents or living with foster parents.

After a while, in a marriage, the euphoria of love fades. It's a natural cycle in every relationship. Slowly but surely, where has the feeling gone? Touching that was once welcome is now not always pleasant. Life is not like a bed of roses anymore when it turns to a briar patch. Things are not as smooth as we expect them to be. The beautiful relationship loses some sparkle. But, people, because of our immature attitude and impatience, fail to keep the desired spark of love alive in marriages today. Why?

Problems originate in marriage because two individuals come together, and clashes are going to take place. Time will bring about changes. What I used to do; I can't do anymore. Don't let a blaze die down to a little spark. Keep the flames burning.

Getting married brings on responsibilities that one must bear. Amidst the day-to-day tensions, sometimes the person is not able to keep up the expectations of his/her partner. But then that does not mean he/she doesn't love his/her partner. We tend to get upset if he or she has different opinions and makes different choices than I would. A word of caution: you have bumped up some of your control issues and trigger a landslide in your marriage.

It not at all about you, it's about both of you. Men tend to drag chains around with balls on the end of what I used to do before the marriage. That's not good anymore, what you used to do. You gave it up when you said, "I do take this woman to be my wife, until death do us part, for better or worse." Husbands don't be the worst thing that ever happens to your wives. And wives, don't be the worst thing that happens to your husbands.

The basis of marriage is not mutual affection or feelings of emotions and passions that we associate with love, but a vocation, a being elected to build together a house for God in this world, to be like the cherubs whose outstretched wings sheltered the ark of the covenant and created a space in which Yahweh could be present. Violet Woodhouse and Lina Guillen, authors of the book *Divorce and Money: How to Make the Best Financial Decisions During Divorce*, tell us, "Sometimes the seraphim may want to close their wings in some marriage situations when there is chaos. A covenant marriage makes it more challenging to get a divorce. A couple in some states must wait two years before proceeding to end a covenant marriage and separate for reasons such as adultery or alcoholism. It is estimated that between 1/2 percent and 3 percent have opted for covenant marriages in states where it is legal. No matter how you feel about divorce from a spiritual point, you cannot ignore its legal and financial consequences.

It only takes a few minutes in front of a witness and someone with authority to declare you legally married. You don't need a cake, champagne; you don't need a room full of spectators, and you don't need music or even a wedding dress. The only thing you need is a lot of nerve and a license, and someone who wants to get married. You anticipate that both of you are madly in love and can't think of living with someone else. The challenge is to ask God to be there with both of you at the beginning and until the end, and until death do you part. Unless the Lord builds your marriage, the couple will labor in vain. Unless the Lord watches over the marriage, the couple stands and waits in vain (Ps. 127:1). Ask that the Lord's eyes remain on you. His eyes are on the sparrow, and I know he watches me.

The present trend of marriage introduces a challenge of trials, tribulations, and high divorce rates. With the divorce rate high, its clear marriage is not what it used to be. Some emerging issues have led marital researchers to determine what has changed about the nature of marriage since the 1970s. Some researchers have blamed the ease with which we can get a divorce. Barbara Whitehead, the author of the book *The Divorce Culture*, tells us, "Divorce is embedded in culture, laws, and institutions. They are also embedded in our manners and mores, movies and television shows, novels, children's storybooks, and in our relationships." Divorce has become deeply entrenched.

Researchers have shown that covenant marriage is fading. Many people have walked, crawled, and run away from the biblical views of marriage as instituted by God between the male and female. Any other way is an evasion of the original process. The modern-day perspective continues to prevail, and the family will suffer a great tragedy. Humanity will experience a great tragedy. Marriage is in trouble because of the alarming numbers of divorces.

The reasonability of marriage is at a time when marriage is devalued, and cohabitation and divorce seem familiar. Families have gone through divorce or relationship breakups after many years of marriage. The quality of commitment has been distorted and scary. Shaunti Feldhahn, a researcher and author of the book *The Good News About Marriage*, was puzzled by all the bad news about marriage. She spent years interviewing other researchers, reviewing the original data, and coming to different conclusions. Some researchers suggest that marriage is facing a divorce rate of 50 percent. She determined 20 to 25 percent for first marriages and 31 percent for all marriages. She also found that:

1. About 80 percent of marriages are happy.

2. Those who acted on faith have the lower divorce rate.

3. Remarriages are only seeing about 30 percent failure (vs. over 60 percent as reported in the media).

We quickly seek a divorce because we find the answer to another dream. The better for the worst is present because I am looking for something better, and this is my fourth wife. We are compunctious to say, "It's my fault; I committed the crime of mistrust."

In the twenty-first century, we have seen dramatic changes in laws relating to marriage. Among the most significant were the no-fault divorce laws passed 30 years ago. These laws made it easier for a husband or wife to walk away from that commitment. In a covenant marriage, you are bound for life. The birth control pill made it easy for unmarried couples to live together, as supposedly, there are no negative consequences to having children. These shifts further diminished the responsibility or obligation to have children.

In Matthew 19, a group of Pharisees approached Jesus and started a debate about marriage, for they were trying to justify their views of divorce and remarriage. Jesus redefined marriage and affirmed God's original intent for marriage. Jesus's view of marriage is between a man and a woman, and he proceeded to call all sexual behavior outside of marriage as sexual immorality (Matt. 19:3–7).

Sexual union outside of the marriage breaks the covenant and is the biblical ground for divorce. There are two biblical reasons for divorce. The first reason is adultery, as Jesus taught in Matthew 19:3–9. The Pharisees also came unto him, tempting him, and saying unto him, "Is it lawful for a man to put away his wife for every cause?" They came to Jesus to tempt him; they did not want to know his reasons for divorce. They were trying to entrap Him in a theological debate. "And they said, Moses suffered to write a bill of divorcement, and to put her away. And Jesus answered and said unto them, For the hardness of your heart he wrote you this precept" (Mk. 10:2). For every reason; is the essence of the argument.

Jesus addressed divorce by quoting from Deuteronomy 24:1 tells us, "When a man hath taken a wife, and married her, and it come to pass that she find no favor in his eyes, because he hath found some uncleanness in her: then let him write her a bill of divorcement, and give it in her hand, and send her out of his house." If a man marries a woman who becomes displeasing to him because he finds something indecent about her, and he writes her a certificate of divorce, gives it to her and sends her from his house. Moses didn't justify divorce, but it regulated the abuses by husbands who divorced their wives. Because of this unfair standard, wives could not divorce their husbands, so giving her "a writing of divorcement" allowed her to remarry as a means of supporting herself (Deut. 24:1).

When the Pharisees asked Jesus why did Moses command to give "a writing of divorcement" to put a wife away, Jesus replied that "Moses because of the hardness of your hearts suffered (allowed) you to put away (divorce) your wives: but from the beginning it was not so" (Matt. 19:7–9). A man could not divorce his wife in order to fulfill his lust for another, he had to do it through a legal document in writing and attested to by witnesses. If the husband was going to dissolve ordained matrimonial bond, he had to do it in writing. As time went on, divorce became very common, and how to do it legally was misunderstood by the Pharisees. They divorced a wife for any reason (Matt. 19:3). Jesus disagreed with this attitude. He declared one justifiable reason for divorce was fornication or marital unfaithfulness. "But I say unto you, that whosoever shall put away his wife, saving for the cause of fornication, cause her to commit adultery: and whosoever shall marry her that is divorced commit adultery (Matt. 5:32). What God had joined together; no man had the right to separate (Matt. 19:6).

Across the country, this is what happens so many times in marriage. One person makes all the decisions, and when there is a decision carried out without the help of the other, all hell breaks out. We get violent like a raging bull, full of fire, and want to burn the house down. We feel trapped because we have lost control. That marriage will not stay together, but will lead to an emotional divorce, which is a tragedy. The first step, the house goes up for sale. Get the problem fixed. Do not practice gaining control.

The marriage that is cracked up, torn up, and in need of desperate repair comes from a lack of cooperation, trust, and respect. The works of indecency described in marriage are manifested because one spouse gets tired of a confrontational situation and wants something different. A man said, "My wife and I had a disagreement when she refused to consult me when she purchased a car." I wanted a divorce because my wife did not ask for assistance because I suggested using the money to pay off debts. She buys the car, and the husband calls the sheriff's department and asks them to convince the wife to return the vehicle to the dealership after she had purchased the car. The wife did ask for his assistance in buying the car. The chemistry will quickly change to adultery, fornication, uncleanness, lasciviousness, fanaticism, hatred, disagreement, emulations, wrath, strife, seditions, heresies, envying, and murder.

Jesus demonstrated that if you discover that your partner has been unfaithful, it is your duty to make every effort to forgive, reconcile, and restore your relationship. You must always look for reasons to restore the marriage relationship rather than look for excuses to leave it. The prophet Malachi reminds Christians that the Lord hates divorce (Mal. 2:15–16).

According to a recent survey of 191 Certified Divorce Financial Analyst professionals from across North America, the three leading causes of divorce are fundamental incompatibility (43 percent), infidelity (28 percent), and money issues (22 percent). Emotional, physical abuse lagged far behind (nearly 6 percent), and parenting issues/arguments, addiction and alcoholism issues received only point 5 percent each.

John Gottman is a highly respected marriage researcher who was able to predict when newly married couples are likely to stay together and those who were expected to split up. His views have become quite prevalent among marriage therapists. He was able to guide the couples with their differences. They can be handled with calm, productive, collaborative talking together that dissipates issues and yields creation of mutually comfortable solutions.

Paul said, "Now the works of the flesh are manifest, which are these; Adultery, fornication, uncleanness, lasciviousness, Idolatry, witchcraft, hatred, variance, emulations, wrath, strife, seditions, and heresies. Envying, murders, drunkenness, reveling, and such like: of the which I tell you before, as I have also told you in time past, that they which do such things shall not inherit the kingdom of God" (Gal. 5:19–21). The works of darkness are shameful; "For it is a shame even to speak of those things which are done of them in secret" (Eph. 5:12). What is done in the dark will come to light.

Researchers have found that children from divorced families become adults who are "more likely to have problems forming relationships and less happy than children who grew up in two-parent families. Problems resulting from children of divorce include:

1. Being disobedient.

2. Staying away from school.

3. Getting bad results at school.

4. Behaving angrily in situations that were completely acceptable for them before the divorce.

5. Avoidance of their social network (which they need).

6. Being depressed.

7. Anxiousness.

8. Blaming themselves for the separation of their parents.

The effects of divorce are primarily the result of dysfunctional families. Children of divorce find it hard to trust other people; they fear intimacy with another would result in more pain.

Matthew Jacobson of *Faithful Men* says, "The more men who love their wives deeply, passionately, and faithfully; more women who are cherished by their husbands; more wives who respect their husbands; more singles who are prepared to be good husbands, wives, moms and dads obedience to the Word of God."

Many children of divorce have "trouble forming romantic relationships in their late 20s and early 30s due to the fear that their relationships would fail. The emotional damage (from childhood divorce) is felt well into the adult years, even taking a toll on educational attainment." Children of divorce are at risk for problems in school. They have more disruptive classroom behavior, are absent more often, as well as have generally lower IQ scores than children from non-divorced families." Children from divorced families were also found to repeat grade levels and have lower academic performance after a divorce had occurred.

Christina D Richardson and Lee A. Rosen tell us, "Emotional support in the school setting is effective in helping children of divorce cope with their situation." Divorce also permanently weakens the family and the relationship between children and parents.

Four out of five children who use drugs and alcohol and come from divorced families admitted that their schoolwork was affected negatively as a result.

Dr. Deborah Khoshaba reported that the family influences the child in many ways. The family serves as a social system that helps the child learn to deal with emotional forces. Parenting styles are related to a variety of developmental outcomes, including academic achievement, social functioning, mental health, and delinquency. Research has also revealed racial and ethnic differences in how parenting style affects children.

A new study of divorce and children confirms the notion that environment strongly influences behavior, but it also finds evidence that parents transmit risk for adjustment problems through their genes. The study tested the hypothesis that genetics can affect how a child copes with divorce. As reported in the current issue of *Developmental Psychology*, the researchers analyzed data on 12-year-olds in 188 adoptive families and 210 biological families. The result, which supports previous findings on divorce and behavior, is consistent with the notion that a child's achievement and social competence are under some genetic influence.

The Bible says that God hates divorce because it destroys the family and the family is the basis of society. It destroys the social fabric. It kills the children like a twisting tornado. Children of divorce have a self-esteem problem, lack of security, and are far more prone to trying separation themselves. They have seen their mother and father could not stick it out. God's message is to work out your problem and stay together.

Fighting, if not managed, will lead to a divorce. When a marriage is devastated with a divorce, it can be described as a catastrophic storm of biblical proportions. "Trust in the LORD with all thine heart; and lean not unto thine own understanding. In all thy ways acknowledge him, and he shall direct thy paths" (Prov. 3:6-7).

CHAPTER SIX

Communication In Marriage

A marriage involves excellent communication to be understood both partners doing everything. Each partner pushes and pulls by the very nature of the relationship to grow as needs are met. The process of communication is never-ending. It is a difficult task to achieve through the sharing of experiences with the other person. A passion and genuine concern for the other is a true mark of excellent communication between the couple. Jerome Nathanson proclaims, "Good communication is a difficult thing to achieve, but through the sharing of experiences can be accomplished.

If you get married, you must master the art of communication. A marriage will only rise to the level of communication that transpires within it. It is not just an expression of great ideal, but an expression and conveyance of your messages. The role of effective communication among married couples cannot be overemphasized. Marital communication skills enable couples to perform proficiently when engaged in the symbolic transfer of messages. What is said, how it is said, and the way it is interpreted are very important factors in effective communication. It is recommended that couples are taught in order to enhance self-disclosure, identify feelings of the other partner and to find out the actual sources of dissatisfaction through the application of the treatments. Communication is not an inborn talent, and it must be practiced.

Before humans developed the ability to communicate with a spoken language, they used body language, such as facial expressions and gestures. Animals use body language to supplement their oral communication. A dog barks and wags his tail. A horse paws the ground. The rattlesnake shakes its tail as a warning to get out of its way.

Two types of communication exist in marriage: verbal communication and visual communication. Men are not good listeners when it comes to listening to their wives. The wife wants you to hear when she has something to say. It is difficult to listen when you are watching your favorite sports team, or the wife is watching her favorite soap opera. Both of you need to pay attention when the other has something to say.

Researchers have estimated that a person is capable of twenty thousand distinct gestures, each having a meaning. Words convey information; nonverbal communications add meaning to the data. The vocal and visual elements of speech are favorable to how the message will be received.

A significant aspect of a covenant marriage is communication. The first step is to hear from God as a counselor. He will inspire, direct, and encourage what you will speak to your spouse. A wise man will hear and increase in learning, and a man of understanding will acquire wise counsel (Prov. 1:4).

In a covenant marriage, communication is the primary source of strength. There must be an effort to bring about meeting between the minds of both spouses. The principles of communication must be employed in a language that can be interpreted with understanding. If that does not happen, look for ways to communicate.

Smiling, nodding your head, even letting your partner know you care in ways of communicating.

When you communicate, do you speak words of wisdom? If your spouse is not walking with Jesus, you may have some problems in communicating. You must live like Christ, think, walk, and talk like Christ. "Let all bitterness, and wrath, and anger, and clamor, and evil speaking, be put away from you, with all malice. And be ye kind one to another, tenderhearted, forgiving one another, even as God for Christ's sake hath forgiven you" (Eph. 4:31-32).

Encourage by praising each uniqueness in conversation. Each of you has differences, and if you do not understand your differences, problems in communicating will affect the outcome of the relationship. A good marriage requires excellent communication between the couple. There are right ways and wrong ways to communicate. Listening without interrupting, not talking too much, and providing the time for communicating is essential. When you live with someone over a long period, it's quite common to stop showing as much appreciation and respect as you did at the beginning of the relationship. By allowing your significant other to speak his or her mind without cutting in or adding your views, you let them know that their opinions are vital (even though you may not agree with them). Always make good comments about your spouse. My wife asked me, "Honey, tell me how I look in this dress." You look great, even though she weighs 300 pounds. People want to feel good about who they are, and your negative comments can destroy their self-esteem.

The body has five senses, and each plays a role for the body to function. In a marriage, some aspects are significant. Some issues to consider are how you look at your marriage (eyes), how you handle your marriage (hands), how you feel about your marriage (heart), how you listen to your wife (ears), and how you talk with understanding (the tongue). Of course, there are many other contributors: Love, respect, knowledge, and dedication. We spend a lot of time on love, primarily when the feeling arises, but we need to learn to love with our ears and eyes. It has been found that happy couples with marital stability and satisfaction were more likely to use active listening skills, agree, approve, assent, use laughter and humor, and possess character virtues of self-restraint, courage, and friendship. Excellent communication is said to be a lifeline of a healthy marriage. "A wise man will hear and will increase learning; and a man of understanding shall attain unto wise counsels" (Prov. 1:5). The power of words in communication is incredibly powerful when spoken.

Death and life are in the power of the tongue: and they that love it shall eat the fruit thereof (Prov. 18:21).

A wholesome tongue is a tree of life: but perverseness therein is a breach in the spirit (Prov. 15:4).

Pleasant words are as a honeycomb, sweet to the soul, and health to the bones (Prov. 16:24).

A word fitly spoken is like apples of gold in pictures of silver (Prov. 25:11).

Words are significant in how they are spoken. A man was sitting in church, and during a sermon, the preacher said, "Everyone is going to die." The preacher noticed that the man began to smile. The pastor found the man and asked, "Why in the world did you smile when I said, 'Every member of this church is going to die?' The man erupted with a huge smile, 'I'm not a member of this church.'"

The most excellent level of communication begins when you share your emotions, talk about your dreams and fears, your love of people and things, about good times. It's time to take off the mask and the makeup, and you are willing to share with your spouse facts, faults, and failures openly without manipulating and trickery. Avoid nagging, as it is one of the worst forms of communication.

Each day I say to my spouse, "I love you, and you're beautiful." Some other important words I have learned to say, when appropriate are, "I'm sorry." Listening is excellent communication. You don't have to solve problems; be an active listener. Turn off the TV, email, the Internet, texting, iPhones, iPods, video games, put down the newspaper, and give your spouse your full attention. The constant flitting back and forth between these media makes it hard to pay attention to things that really matter.

An old proverb says, "Sticks and stone may break my bones, but names will never hurt me." That's not true. That is a silly lie because words will hurt. James says, "Even so the tongue is a little member, and boast great things. Behold, how great a matter a little fire kindle! And the tongue is a fire, a world of iniquity so is the tongue among our members, that it defiles the whole body, and set on fire the course of nature; and it is set on fire of hell. (Jas. 3:5–6). James also says, "But the tongue can no man tame; it is an unruly evil, full of deadly poison" (Jas. 3:8). Mr. Tongue can claw your mate and kill her with words.

Each person must learn to control the tongue. I believe the tongue is filled with rattlesnake poison and is deadlier than bullets when dirty words like profanity, curses, obscenities are fired at your spouse. When it strikes, it will destroy the nerve and emotions. What you have built up for years in the character of your marriage can be torn apart in striking out with some bad words. I am careful when I hear a torching tongue, a tiger tongue, or a rattlesnake tongue, used by anyone, but when spouses put some poison in their tea, the marriages will find no antidote for a torching tongue. Communication will fall apart.

When it comes to communication, most women expect men to get distracted, defensive, irritated, fidgety, or shut down entirely because they feel punished for a crime they did not commit. Women like kind and sweet words. Researchers have discovered that the chance of men talking about a problem is more of a chance of making it worse. Women love for men to explain the details. Men would rather eat dirt than to talk about problems or issues in marriage. Women want to talk, and men don't want to talk. So, this creates loneliness of disconnection in every argument, and fuels disappointment or resentment.

The difference between male and female communication is that women want all the information and details explained. Men want to be left alone and explain a few details. He began to look at this kind of behavior as nagging. It is an enemy of excellent communication. The couple needs to work out the barriers of communication. Spouses should seek to understand each other in mutual understanding with the heart of love. Josh McDowell, the author of the book *The Secrets of Loving*, recommends:

- Work it out.
- Learn to compromise.
- Seek to understand.
- Affirm the worth, dignity, and value your spouse.
- Always be positive and encouraging.
- Practice communications skills (affection, listening, talking about the problems, avoid criticisms, threats, intimidation, be honest).

Most problems of communication start when there is a sense of disconnection because of poor communication; spouses have poor communication because they are disconnected. Women process information by their emotional brains and can be logical and sensitive at the same time. Men are more likely to use one side of the brain at a time. Understand your differences and seek God and ask for ways to communicate that will turn your marriage into a roaring success.

Communication barriers are created because of the difference between each spouse and how we communicate. A barrier of communication is styles. They are determined by many influences, including culture, gender, and upbringing. Sometimes, style differences rooted in family backgrounds can cause great misunderstandings, becoming powerful filters that distort communication.

Power struggles happen when two people fight to protect themselves from shame or fear. She wants him to do what she wants so she doesn't feel like a failure. They control each other with pressuring the other to submit. More resentment and hostility occur when their rights are not filled, and communication barriers are created. Whatever you want, you are out to prove it. If you were a good spouse, you wouldn't have to prove anything. He will do for you because he loves you, you feel connected and thereby reduce the fear of isolation and deprivation.

The principles that can help marriages grow and increase marital happiness are understanding, love for each other, and a sense of fulfillment and to keep unwanted people out of the marital life and enjoying more interpersonal quality time together.

CHAPTER SEVEN

The Condition of Good Marriage

The conditions of marriage depend on the person you are asking. From a secular view, marriage is made up of love, trust, honesty, and understanding. Spiritually, there is an added element of faith in God's hands to build each relationship with agape love. A marriage established on agape love will keep the marriage with fire long after the physical attraction has gone out. God will bless those who follow His plan of marriage.

In comparing the views of marriage, we can see that there are similarities and differences. When marriage is viewed from a religious perspective, we see marriage in the context of faith and a relationship with God. The couple is to submit themselves in conversation and sacrificial love toward each other, as Christ loved the Church. Marriages deeply rooted in a secular plan (same-sex marriage) will not work to start a family. In a covenant marriage, the man is the head of the family, and the wife is designated as a helper as she submits to her husband (Gen. 2:18). A marriage is characterized by genuine concerned to produce offspring in the image of God.

When you were dating, you did not think about someone to take care of you and trust you. You looked for somebody romantic, which was the fun part of the relationship. When you began to look for someone to marry, you began to face reality with wanting to find someone you can argue with when the bills come, disciplining children, and someone for me.

A young man or woman who leaves the adolescent stage dominated with inferiority complexes and role confusion will also have difficulty with intimacy. They will feel more comfortable isolated in their ego boundaries. Isolation is their safety net from a society where they are not able to attain satisfaction for their need for social acceptance. Intimacy is the bedrock for a happy marriage.

Each person signs a contract and learns to contribute money, property, skills, and sharing in the process of better or worse. All profits are used to pay for food, shelter, protection, education, health, clothing, transportation, investment, and the basic needs of the family. Marriage is for life, and the idea of withdrawing becomes an unfavorable condition.

Does this mean that your mate is a dictator? Any husband who thinks this way needs to learn how Jesus made His Bride submissive by loving and dying for her. If you are a husband, you gave up your rights to a spouse. No longer can you make decisions based merely upon what you want. Her welfare must be considered. You are to love your wife, magnanimously, gallantly, and courteously. Husbands are to love their wives just like Jesus loved the Church, and He gave His life for the Church (Eph. 5:25). The husband provides for the wife's needs as it pleases your own body. The more you give, the more you're going to get. Be kind to your wife like you love yourself.

The Lord teaches that wives are to submit to their husbands not as a slave, but as a loving woman. Why does God instruct women in this way? Because He has a chain of command. Most men are stronger than most women and it is the difference between Beauty and the Beast.

The job that God gave to Adam was two-fold; to be the provider and the protector. Eve is to become the life-giver. She is made to nurture, to love, to be gentle, to be soft, and to be cuddly. Women are lovers, and men are achievers. The most profound need for a woman is romance. The greatest need of a man is to be admired and respected. A woman is infinitely superior over a man when it comes to be a woman. The man is infinitely superior to a woman at being a man.

And in the sight of God, they are complete equals (Gal. 3:28). If the man does not take care of his wife, and the wife does not submit to the husband, they are going to have serious problems.

The first problem is a spiritual problem. God is the One who told her to submit. Secondly, the husband is going to have a problem because he will not be able to assume God's role as head of the family and provide the character of Jesus.

Jesus provided for the Church, and the husband provides for his wife. The husband meets the wife's needs by assuming his role as her provider, protector, priest, and prayer warrior. To marry means giving up some of your rights to your spouse. No longer can you make decisions based upon what you want. The wife's welfare must be considered, and she cannot become selfish. Husbands are to love their wives (see Eph. 5:25).

The husband is the prophet and priest of the family who offers prayers and teaching the word of God to his family. Husbands are to love their wives supremely (see Eph. 5:28). Earthly relationships end, including his parents, sisters, brothers, and he loves and cleaves to his wife above his parents, sisters, brothers, friends, business, and hobbies. The same is expected of the wife that is expected of the husband. No other institution exists that is more significant than marriage because it is the highest of all human relationships.

Marriage is not just a force of nature, but it can be like a ship in a storm. Marriage is not all pleasure, passion, but compassion for one to the other. It is a union of coming together for better or worse until death do you part. One of the dangers of marriage is being committed to different things and not confined to your wife in everything, which includes other people.

Marriages are either good or bad, depending on how much you are willing to invest; that is, your whole life. You are going to have strengths and weaknesses. No marriage is perfect. Every marriage deteriorates to the point of dying unless we want it to grow. Fight or fuss, but you must amend because you are going to have some severe problems. A good definition of the good of marriage is knowing how to fix your pressing issues. A good marriage has problems because we are humans. What makes a bad marriage is you not willing to compromise. A bad marriage is one where the relationship has been, and the couple lives in the same house with a different address.

Jerome Nathanson in an article titled "The Ethics of Marriage," outlines the conditions of a good marriage in context. The author names three needs marriage fulfills: security, understanding, and genuine concern for your partner. The requirement for safety can be satisfied if there is a "profound awareness that no matter what happens, you can always feel completely at home." No matter what ups and downs outside or within the home, you can count on your spouse. Another aspect of a good marriage is the sense of security and the mutual dependence in which each partner can rely on the support and assistance in return. The other needs to be understood.

Marriage is more than sexual passion, which has nothing whatever to do with love. Each partner is pushed and pulled in the relationship to grow and meet the needs of their mate. This process is never finished and is always a work in construction. If your marriage is going to be successful, you will need Jesus to work in your relationship daily. Marriage should contain a little of heaven.

Marriage should be a couple making contributions to the life of the other. A secular intimacy without a spiritual inspiration can be compared to two people living together without check and balance, and the similarities are very evident.

When you get married, you bring to the table your rights, and she brings her rights. God made man head of the family. He does not come into the marriage with a buckle of rights, thinking he can do a better job than his spouse. He may bring along weeds that need to be cultivated along with the crop. Marriage is like growing a new crop. You fight to keep the weeds out. If the couple continues to let the grass grow, the marriage will fail, and your marriage will be in chaos. Marriages are failing today because there is no commitment to allow partners to grow. Some marriages fail because of the following reasons:

- My spouse corrects me all the time with negative comments and tells me I am wrong.

- My spouse challenges things I say, questioning their truth before I complete a sentence.

- My spouse refuses to let me defend my actions and tends to become angry about some subjects.

- My spouse spends no time with me going out to dinner, the movies, and other social activities.

- My spouse is continually criticizing my family, friends, relatives, and coworkers.

- My spouse is always complaining about financial matters.

- My spouse spends too much time talking with family members and following their guidance.

- My spouse is always egotistical and full of pride.

A woman happened to run into the famous painter Picasso at a restaurant, and so boldly she approached the master and asked him if he would please scribble something on her napkin, saying she would be happy to pay him whatever he felt the quick drawing would be worth. Picasso took her napkin and drew something and handed it to her, adding, "That, my fine lady, will be 10,000 dollars!" The stunned woman then said, "But you did that drawing in barely 30 seconds!" Picasso answered, "No, it has taken me 40 years to do that!" – Source unknown.

Paul stresses the husband should be concerned about his wife's spiritual growth as Christ is for the Church. He quoted that the husband and wife become one flesh through marriage (Gen. 2:24). Christ gave himself for the Church (Eph. 5:25). When a man loves his wife, he loves himself. The relationship is so deep that they are a single being. That love is called agape, referring to giving love that seeks the highest good for the other.

A Christian husband and father's duties are to serve his spouse and to remain faithful in a lifelong commitment to her. He is to meet his wife's sexual needs (1 Cor. 7:3). The husband loves his wife as he loves himself (Eph. 5:25). He brings up his children in training and instructions of the Lord (Eph. 6:4). He provides for the material needs of the family (1 Tim. 5:8).

Christian wives and mothers are to remain faithful to their husbands in a lifelong commitment. She is to meet her husband's sexual needs (1 Cor. 7:3). The wife submits to the husband's leadership role in the home (Eph. 5:22-24). She is to respect her husband and develops an inward charm and beauty.

The wife's duty is to be a helpmate to her husband. They expect the grace of God is with them until death. A great relationship depends on a great meeting of the minds. I am convinced that nothing can ever separate the precious love of a husband and wife. Neither death, life, angels, demons, fears, worries, or the powers of hell can separate your love for each other if it is genuine love. No power in the world above or in the earth below, nothing in all creation will ever be able to separate your love from your spouse. Husband love your wife like Christ loved the Church, and the spouse is encouraged to love your husband, just like your husband loves Christ (Eph. 5:25). Paul so beautifully wrote these words:

Charity suffer long and is kind; charity envy not; charity vaunt not itself, is not puffed up, doth not behave itself unseemly, seek not her own, is not easily provoked, thinketh no evil; rejoice not in iniquity, but rejoice in the truth. Bear all things, believeth all things, hope all things, endure all things. Love is always patient and kind. It is never jealous. And now abide faith, hope, charity, these three; but the greatest of these is charity (1 Cor. 13:4–7,13).

Love is never boastful or conceited; it is never rude or selfish; it does not take offense and is not resentful. Love takes no pleasure in other people's sins but delights in the truth; it is always ready to excuse, to trust, to hope, and to endure whatever comes. Love does not come to an end. In short, three things last: faith, hope, and love. The greatest of these is love (1 Cor. 13:4–7,13).

My marriage is still under construction. I recommend doing three simple activities that can help you keep yours alive.

1. When was the last time you surprised your spouse with a kiss? Catch him off guard in a pleasant way. A little kiss can instantly make your spouse feel wanted and attractive and make it a habit.

2. I like to reach out and touch my spouse daily. It can be a full body hug, holding hands, or even just putting an arm around a shoulder. I love to be a funny comedian. Don't be a dull person, and don't be so severe.

3. Make sure these activities are done daily: listening, kissing, and touching your partner each day can have profound effects on a relationship.

Marriage is a serious business, and you should work to improve it daily. The old ship of matrimony is sailing through some troubled seas these days with couples jumping overboard every day, but that can be averted. Many will stay chained to the marriage for the children, business, social pressure, or even connected to the Church, but they won't enjoy the trip. A failing marriage is not a good thing. God intends for us to have a good marriage created from the true fellowship of the wife and the loving leadership of her husband in the name of the Father, the Son, and the Holy Spirit.

When you trust someone with your life, they should be faithful to you.

And while he yet spoke, lo, Judas, one of the twelve, came, and with him a great multitude with swords and staves, from the chief priests and elders of the people. Now he that betrayed him gave them a sign, saying, Whomsoever I shall kiss, that same is he: hold him fast. (Matt. 26:47–49).

How do you keep the "honey" in your marriage? How do you keep the excitement and the thrill going? How do you continue to trust your mate in all circumstances? The following illustration demonstrates how much you love your wife.

A husband and wife were attending a county fair where for five dollars, a man was giving rides on an old biplane. The couple wanted to go up, but they thought the price was too steep. Consequently, they tried to negotiate a lower price. "We'll pay you five dollars for both of us," they said to the pilot. "After all, we'll both have to squeeze into that tiny cockpit that was built for only one person." The pilot refused to lower his price, but he made a counteroffer. He said to the couple, "Pay me the full price of ten dollars, and I will take you up. And if you don't say one word during the flight, I will give you all your money back." The couple agreed and got into the plane. Up they went, and the pilot proceeded to perform every trick he knew, looping and whirling and flying upside down and lots more. Finally, when the plane had landed, the pilot said to the husband, "Congratulations! Here are your ten dollars; you didn't say a single word." To which the man replied, "Nope, but I almost did when my wife fell out."

Marriage loses its honeymoon luster in about seven years, and the thing will start to turn around. How you handle matters will determine the future.

Dr. Adrian Rogers recommends the seven characters that will destroy your marriage.

- Don't play the judge who condemns and declares someone to be guilty.
- Don't play the professor who likes to talk down their victim.
- Don't use constant belittling attacks.
- Don't be a psychologist who regularly analyzes and assigns their mate's justified motives.
- Don't be the historian who brings up everything out of the past and resurrects old things.
- Don't play the dictator who likes to use force.
- Don't use negative words and physical force to rob your partner of self-esteem.

- Don't play the critic who condemns and criticizes their spouse, comparing them with somebody else.

- Don't play the preacher who takes the role of pastor or priest and uses the Bible as a club to beat their spouse's conscience with the word of God to direct the behavior when they are wrong.

Behavior in a marriage is centered around what is wrong. When the body is sick it is because something is illegal in the system. They become the flesh of my flesh and bones of my bones. Both of you know that something is wrong, but you tend to back off and retreat. You pretend to the world there is nothing wrong. Some spouses retreat because they fear their partner will become angry and rebel with harsh words or shut down with cruel treatment. Sometimes one spouse will say nothing is wrong when the marriage is falling apart. They live in the same house, but they are in the world alone in their relationship. Sometimes we are afraid to speak because we are going get into an argument. Sometimes we are scared to get into an argument because my mate is going to be abusive. To resolve a conflict, I have suggested going to a counselor, but they admitted nothing is wrong. You may stuff it, you may repress it, but the stomach, head, body, and nerve will keep score. Your marriage problem cannot be placed on the shelf and you refuse to accept it; seek help. Your problem will crawl around the house and return through the basement window. Don't practice avoidance; ask for help. The rule of confrontation is to love your mate enough to confront the problem and seek immediate resolution.

Some mates never compromise or applaud their mate when both work and earn a salary. They appease themselves by pointing the finger at their partner when things don't go their way. One person always finds a reason to complain that's not my fault, so why should I compromise? One person seems always to be in control and get away with it because they accuse the other of wrong. Never are there compromises in the situation. The agreement means both of you get or give in the argument.

Here are some ways to bond with your spouse.

1. Go out on dates, take the time to get away just to be with your spouse.

2. Say things about your spouse above others. Never put your spouse down in the public, even if you don't agree.

3. Compliment your spouse. Thank him or her for the big things done and be excited when you give thanks. Man thrives on appreciation.

4. You work hard to accomplish things to make family proud. Make sure you stop and notice those things. Strive to see things from each other's perspective.

5. Tell your spouse verbally several times a day how much you love them. Flirt with your spouse and do things to get him in order to keep him.

Marriage is shared in the control tower without practicing aggressiveness. Marriage takes a lot of effort, and it becomes the responsibility of both partners. Even though you have signed a contract and executed a pledge, oath, declaration, and undertaking, you must keep working every day to keep the ruff, bumps, holes, and trap contained or repaired. Marriage is like construction work; you've got to keep building and building until it develops into a lovely, beautiful, and precious thing. Don't let your marriage lose its invigorating source of affection. The following illustration from *The Seven Ages of the Married Cold* is shared for your pleasure and can be a beautifully used source to check yourself as often as you can.

Frist Year - The husband says, Oh, sweetie pie, I'm apprehensive about those nasty sniffles you have! There's no telling what that could turn into with all the strep throat that's been going around. I'm going to take you right down to the hospital and have you admitted for a couple of days of rest. I know the food is lousy there, so I'm going to bring you some takeout from China Garden. I've already arranged it with the head nurse.

Second Year - Listen, honey, I don't like the sound of that cough. I called the doc, and he's going to stop by here and look at you. Why don't you go on to bed and get the rest you need?

Third Year - Maybe you'd better lie down, darling. When you feel lousy, you need the rest. I'll bring you something to eat. Do we have any canned soup around here?

Fourth Year - Honey, there is no sense wearing yourself out when you're under the weather. When you finish those dishes and the kids' baths and get them to bed, you ought to go to sleep.

Fifth year - Why don't you take a couple of aspirin?

Sixth Year - You ought to go gargle or something, instead of sitting around barking like a dog.

Seventh Year - Stop sneezing. Are you trying to give me pneumonia? You'd better pick up some tissues while you're at the store.

CHAPTER EIGHT

Same-Sex Marriage

The world has defined God's message of covenant marriage as backward, old-fashioned, and out of step with time. God's precepts of a covenant marriage are suitable for the fullness of times: spiritual and instructional. God has put everything in place, and now, Satan comes to destroy God's plan. Secularization in our culture has created a non-Christian culture dominated with humanistic and moralities that is man centered. There is no limit to what humanity will develop as a yearning for desires. Satan seeks every opportunity to destroy covenant marriage. Every chance to destroy the family. He attempts to strip covenant marriage of wealth and value with his power and cunning. The saddest thing on earth is for marriage to become shipwrecked by satanic intrinsic worth. It is tragic to witness wasted talent and lost lives set on a road of devastation. Covenant marriage must continue to take a walk with God.

Satan continues to use what seems to be harmless fruit that appeals to human desire. Anything that seems forbidden is something that humanity has lusted over. The word *lust* means a strong passion for something that tempts an appetite of pleasure. Temptation has to do with the action that attracts a desire. "Now the works of the flesh are manifest, which are these; adultery, fornication, uncleanness, lasciviousness, Idolatry, witchcraft, hatred, variance, emulations, wrath, strife, seditions, heresies, envying, murders, drunkenness, reveling, and such like: of the which I tell you before, as I have also told you in time past, that they which do such things shall not inherit the kingdom of God" (Gal. 5:19–21).

You are warned to flee from immorality. Every sin that a man commits is a sin against his body. "What? know ye not that your body is the temple of the Holy Ghost, which is in you, which ye have of God, and ye are not your own? For ye are bought with a price: therefore, glorify God in your body, and in your spirit, which are God's" (1 Cor. 6:19–20).

Satan appealed to the lust of the flesh and caused Eve to partake of the forbidden fruit. Adam and Eve sinned when they disobeyed the clear command of God (Gen. 3:6). Because of their transgression, they faced physical and spiritual death, banishment from the presence of the Lord, as well as temporal death. The spiritual death came at the time of the fall and banishment from the garden (Gen. 3:23–24). The seeds of the physical destruction were also sown at that same time; that is, a physical change came subject to the ills of the flesh, which resulted in their gradual decline of longevity, and finally the separation of the Spirit of God from the body.

Today, we have concluded that if a person lusts for something, we ought to let them have it. A man lusts for naked women. Just click on those internet pictures. A person lusts for a high. We legalize marijuana. A person married lusts for someone they're not married to. Divorce is the easy and accepted way out. A person lusts to become the sex they were not born. We think they ought to be allowed to change. We legal same-sex marriage.

God created Adam, and He created Eve. He did not create another Eve for Eve or Adam for Adam. God created a perfect partnership with some level of difference, as well as a level of similarity. Bones of my bones and flesh of my flesh, the first words that Adam said when he first saw Eve (Gen. 2:23). Adam is complete with her. In the music of marriage, Adam is the violin, and Eve is the bow. Together they make good music. She is complete with Adam. Together they are made for each other. God did not grant her to take the initiative to lead. God gave the man to do that. Christ takes the initiative as the head of the Church.

Some people think that if we do that one little thing we want to do, then our lustful appetite will stop bothering us and life will be okay. Our society lusts and wants for more desires. Proverbs 27 tells us, "Hell and destruction are never full; so, the eyes of man are never satisfied." Just as death and destruction are never satisfied, so human desire is never satisfied. Humanity has reached a point where you begin to wonder if maybe it is beyond reasoning.

Satan has persuaded humanity to stir up a spirit of discontentment. No one can improve on the Christian standard of marriage. Some people have developed their standards of marriage versus that of God. You need the wisdom of the Scripture to transform covenant marriage from a lackluster covenant into an intimate and exciting relationship.

"Wherefore seeing we also are compassed about with so great a cloud of witnesses, let us lay aside every weight, and the sin which doth so easily beset us, and let us run with patience the race that is set before us" (Heb. 12:1). When we run the race of life with endurance, it doesn't take long before the honeymoon is over, or celebrating your golden anniversary, you must remain committed to the intimacy in marriage that God made possible.

Marriage was formerly an institution that secured its members' position both financially and socially and united people who love each other. Sexual intimacy between a man and a woman is the only method of marriage bonding emotional and physical attributes designed for the bodies to be used in the way offspring are produced. God designed the male and female to allow reproduction through sexual intercourse, which would be healthy and natural. "And likewise, also the men, leaving the natural use of the woman, burned in their lust one toward another; men with men working that which is unseemly, and receiving in themselves that recompence of their error which was meet" (Rom. 1:27). Sexual intercourse beyond the natural use carries a high risk of diseases, and this is recognized in Scripture.

Relativism is the most common idea that you do what you desire if you use your set of rules. Some contemporary secular marriages often seek to do what the people want and believe this is what God desires. Same-sex marriage is not right with God and only one can achieve for humanity. The stronger horse wins but at the expense of the weaker one being dragged behind defeated and discouraged. The danger of marriage without God guarantees failure, especially to those that do not embrace God's autonomy in marriage. Marriage is in trouble today, and we need divine guidance. You will be held accountable for your decisions.

Same-sex marriage redefines the definition of marriage, which is also referred to as "traditional marriage." In 2003, Massachusetts was the first state to legalize same-sex marriage. In May 2004, Massachusetts began allowing same-sex couples to marry, giving them spousal benefits and parenting rights.

The *New York Times* reported a recent argument during a debate over whether Massachusetts should ban same-sex marriage by a state constitutional amendment. President Obama stated for many years that he opposed same-sex marriage but supported civil unions. Later he said his opinion was evolving, and in May 2012, he expressed his support of gay marriage. President Obama said, "I think same-sex couples should be able to get married." In December 2012, the Senate passed a bill repealing "Don't ask, don't tell," and President Obama later signed. In 2013, the DOMA was challenged under the federal Constitution in Windsor v. United States. On June 26, 2015, the U.S. Supreme Court ruled all states' bans on same-sex marriage were unconstitutional, allowing gays to marry.

In 1996, President Bill Clinton signed the Defense of Marriage Act (DOMA) into law. DOMA defines marriage as a legal union between one man and one woman. The act gives the authority to make their own rulings about same-sex marriage.

A Gallup Poll found that those who approve of same-sex marriage had reached about 63 percent in 2017, and more than 67 percent (two out of three) in 2018. It includes 83 percent of Democrats, 71 percent of Independents, and 44 percent of Republicans. Adolescents currently in high schools are the first generation to have close friendships with gays/lesbians. They are reaching an understanding of sexual orientation that is far superior to previous generations. Future generations' support for same-sex marriage can only increase as these students age.

Today, so many have documented same-sex marriage is contrary to religious traditions, cultural backgrounds, and parenting concerns. However, research on the importance of marriage stresses the importance of a historical and practical perspective and by legal and political correctness crafted by state legislators that litigated a privilege between the same gender to get married.

Tradition, family, and morality are intimately connected in this analysis, as tradition and family are considered institutions that foster and promote honesty of covenant marriage. Many proponents argue that same-sex marriage denies same-sex couples the right to marry and breaks the equal protection clause of the 14th Amendment, which states, "No state shall make or enforce any law which shall abridge the privileges or immunities of citizens of the United States; nor shall any state deprive any person of life, liberty, or property, without due process of law; nor deny to any person within its jurisdiction the equal protection of the laws."

The argument of same-sex marriage was successful by taking a logical approach to an emotional issue. It did not make biblical claims acceptable but included the argumentative views of constitutional laws.

The tradition frame is the most common that captures the historical context of marriage explicitly as a traditional heterosexual institution. A revolutionizing aspect of including same-sex marriage in the traditional structure of marriage is irrelevant. Many of these conceptualized issues of same-sex marriage are an attack on a God-given principle and a practice that would offend the religious and moral sensibilities of many.

"But as the days of Noe were, so shall also the coming of the Son of man be. For as in the days that were before the flood they were eating and drinking, marrying and giving in marriage, until the day that Noe entered into the ark, and knew not until the flood came, and took them all away; so shall also the coming of the Son of man be" (Matt. 24:37–39). Judah built shrines for male prostitutes in the land and engaged in all the detestable practices of sexuality. It stirred up the Lord's jealous anger against the nations and the Lord cast them out before the Israelites (1 Kings 14:22,24). That is how it's going be at the coming of the Son of man if humanity continues the course.

Paul speaks of homosexuality as a direct result of worshiping idol gods. That would agree with the Old Testament writings of male shrine prostitutes. Paul said that it was degrading, shameful, unnatural, and indecent. "Because that, when they knew God, they glorified him not as God, neither were thankful; but became vain in their imaginations, and their foolish heart was darkened. Professing themselves to be wise, they became fools, and changed the glory of the uncorruptible God into an image made like to corruptible man, and to birds, and four-footed beasts, and creeping things. Wherefore God also gave them up to uncleanness through the lusts of their own hearts, to dishonor their own bodies between themselves" (Rom. 1:22–24). Paul see this as a temptation. When you yield to temptation, God sees that as an act of evil. Therefore, you deprive yourselves of the mercy and grace of God. James tells us, "But every man is tempted, when he is drawn away of his own lust, and enticed" (Jas. 1:13–15). Humans are tempted by their evil desires, which drags them away and entices them. "Then when lust hath conceived, it bringeth forth sin: and sin, when it is finished, bringeth forth death" (Jas. 1:13–15).

Jesus said, ""The lamp of the body is the eye. If therefore your eye is good, your whole body will be full of light. But if your eye is bad, your whole body will be full of darkness. If therefore the light that is in you is darkness, how great is that darkness!" (Matt. 6:22-23). If your eye causes you to sin, gouge it out and throw it away. It is better for you to enter heaven with one eye than to have two eyes and be thrown into the fire of hell (Matt. 18:9). God knows if a person is sincere in their efforts to ask for forgiveness. "If we confess our sins, he is faithful and just to forgive us our sins, and to cleanse us from all unrighteousness" (1 Jn. 1:9). Gay marriage is morally wrong and violates the divine institution of marriage, and those involved should repent and ask for forgiveness.

God warns us in Leviticus 20 that if a man lies with a man as one who lies with a woman, both have done what is repulsive and revolting. God is saying that homosexuality or same-sex marriage is a sin and an abomination (Lev. 20:13). If the Bible speaks the truth, how can anyone deviate the meaning of the Scriptures? The biblical passage in 1 Corinthians 6:9–10 tells us, "Know ye not that the unrighteous shall not inherit the kingdom of God? Be not deceived: neither fornicators, nor idolaters, nor adulterers, nor effeminate, nor abusers of themselves with mankind."

Covenant marriage affirms God's desires for marriage. I oppose the idea of same-sex marriage because of my religious beliefs. Same-sex marriages will lead humanity to devastation, separation from the grace of God, and wrath. Pat Robertson of *The 700 Club Ministries* warned that the Supreme Court would strike down bans on same-sex marriage. He claimed that Christians in America will be attacked like the days of Sodom, when gay men nearly raped angels. He predicted that Christians would be attacked for their beliefs against same-sex marriages. That is already occurring in America.

Same-sex marriage is wrong, according to God's word. God's design for marriage is heterosexual. God has defined marriage as a special covenant relationship between one male and one female. When we redefine marriage and its purpose, then our lives, along with society, will be held accountable. We can only add to an existing saga.

Israel "voted" not to go on into the promised land, trying to overrule the divine agenda and in doing so, chose to become a monarchy when God desired it to become a theocracy (1 Sam. 8:7, 22).

The Church argues that same-sex marriages may deprive some children of the right of having either a natural mother or a father. For instance, the Catholics say that same-sex marriage would erode religious freedoms and that it is contrary to God's will and encourages unhealthy behavior. Same-sex marriage harms the family and increases the dominance of gay behavior; therefore, individuals would act upon their sexual demands. Christians believe that such individuals should seek help to overcome the temptation toward the practice of same-sex marriage. Same-sex relationships are fundamentally different from covenant marriage in respect to spiritual and physical equalities in the essence of God.

Researchers posed some questions to participants in a poll as to whether same-sex marriage should or should not be recognized legally; the responses were collected from Gallup, the Pew Research Center, and *Newsweek* in 1996. All the polls had over 50 percent of the samples rejecting the legality of same-sex marriage, and two of the three polls reported over 60 percent opposed, signifying the public's disagreement with legalizing same-sex marriage. Some data from the study reflected the following results:

The Gallup Poll: Do you think marriages between gays should or should not be recognized by the law as valid, with the same rights as traditional marriages? The factual data (27 percent). Should not be accurate (68 percent). No Opinion (5 percent). The number of participants - 1,008, and the dates of the poll (3/15–17/96).

The Pew Research Center: Do you strongly favor, favor, oppose, or strongly oppose allowing gays and lesbians to marry legally? Data favor (27 percent). Oppose (65 percent). Don't Know (8 percent). The number of participants – 1,975, and the dates of the poll (5/31–6/9/96).

Newsweek: Do you think there should be or should not be legally sanctioned in gay marriage? The data favor (33 percent). Should not (58 percent). Don't know (9 percent). The number of participants - 779, and the dates of the poll (5/22–23/96).

In today's troubled the world of fast food and quick fixes, humanity's persistence in same-sex marriage can be a challenge. Godly marriages must become a high priority. Once you have your heart in the right place before the Lord, He will give you direction to accomplish his will for marriage. Ask God how you can be part of the solution and not a part of the problem. Marriage involves praising God and acknowledging His absolute authority afresh over covenant marriage.

Same-sex marriage couples share the same benefits as covenant marriage: tax filing jointly as a couple, joint ownership, and the ability to make medical decisions for each other. Health care is the other fundamental right that is the same. In a jurisdiction with legal authority to authorize same-sex marriage, an insurance company can't discriminate against them when offering coverage.

Every citizen has the right and privilege to access health care services in the country. The insurance company must provide the same coverage for same-sex couples it provides to opposite-sex spouses in the states where the plan is sold, issued, renewed, or in effect.

They are eligible for any medical care and Medicaid treated in a civil union. They are not allowed to make any critical decision about the other partner in cases of life and death. Furthermore, only a legal parent or family member can make decisions during a health crisis because their marriage is not recognized.

Taxes have also been a pertinent issue for the same sex married citizens of the United States of America. Married couples can file their tax returns jointly; the same now is a constitution right in some states. Married people are eligible to take advantages of the tax benefits that come with filing jointly with exemptions. Same-sex couples now enjoy the same privileges and can take advantage of spousal and survivor benefits. The partners also have no problem transferring their personal property, making it easy for some legal transactions.

During the time of death, same-sex couples suffer a series of grief ranging from being given leave for work to being allowed to take over the ownership of the properties. As it is common among legally wedded couples, the husband or the wife is entitled to a bereavement leave from work. They are given the same rights to inherit any properties that were personally owned by the deceased partner in some states. However, couples must make legal transactions to avoid a disaster.

Immigration problems have been eliminated. The immigration laws recognize same-sex marriages as a legal union and share the same privileges as married couples. They are now allowed to purchase joint homeowner's insurance and auto insurance.

The government has removed issues in many areas that once effected same sex married couples. People who want to get married don't have to fear the consequences which were shared by society. But it continues to threaten and divide the nation and gives a whole new meaning to human sexuality. The Anglican Church has witnessed where the clergy had different stands on the matter, resulting in a split of the Church. Whichever perspective one takes, liberal, conservative, religious, moral, or cultural, a compromise must be reached on the matter as it has a direct bearing on the family unit, and to avoid splits within society. The Church, media, and government working together must play their respective roles to bring an end to same-sex marriage.

Therefore, Christians must seek to be directed by God in marriage and be led by the Holy Spirit. When we decide to get married, we must ask God to direct us, plan, and bless the union of a male and female. Otherwise, we can take a poll on voting down or vetoing what the Scriptures say about marriage when we choose the route of same-sex marriage. Humanity then overrides the master plan of marriage, what is taught by the word of God about marriage, and made it a democracy, when it is a theocracy, thus causing a gift of marriage to humanity to be taken for granted and mistreated.

Like a bright light, same-sex marriage is a deceptive idea darting through the Black Sea of time in a midnight gale coming to destroy the fabric of society and ultimately the Church with laws that often have broad public approval where many people once held conservative religious views as morally right. The Church has been defaced; that is equal to removing the cross lights from which God's precepts have been viewed and practiced from the beginning of covenant marriage between Adam and Eve. It was only by diligent effort and a series of systematic enforcement of constitutional rights that the impossible mission became possible.

Romans 12:2 states, "And be not conformed to this world: but be ye transformed by the renewing of your mind, that ye may prove what is that good, and acceptable, and perfect, will of God." First Corinthians 2:14 tells us, "But the natural man receives not the things of the Spirit of God: for they are foolishness unto him: neither can he know them, because they are spiritually discerned." The natural man cannot grasp spiritual things. There are three essential facts worth perceiving: activating the Holy Spirit to receive the word of God, renewing the mind, and letting go of the arrogant, self-serving intellect that is controlling the body senses.

God does not mention in Scripture that marriage involves anything other than a male and a female. Same-sex marriages are against God's principle of the union of one man and one woman in a fulfilling covenant marriage. A family cannot be formed from the same gender and expect to be fruitful, multiply, and fill the earth (Gen. 1:28).

God's design for the family unit is when a man and woman come together in a sexual relationship and have children. Our whole purpose of life is to glorify God and to enjoy him forever. We live to glorify God in everything. That brings us face-to-face with marriage. What is wrong with so many of us? In all of life, nothing is as important as God, family, and the Church. We miss the one thing, which is the chief plan of God. Marriage another way is wrong. To pay God the ultimate compliment of referring to him in terms of honor and majesty that is always due his name, you do it His way.

We are often exposed to principles that support the role of women as equal to men. The need for a helper has become an obsolete prototype. The husband and wife relation become God's trademark for what He is willing to bless, protect, and supply the needs. Adultery, fornication, same-sex marriage, pornography, polygamy, and divorce are utterly unacceptable without remorse. Couples who live apart from God's design in marriage will suffer pain, loneliness, emotional hardness, physical, and spiritual collapse.

Same-sex marriages refer to all forms of marriage unions whereby persons of similar gender or sex get married and form a family unit, as would a man with a woman in a traditional marriage setup which is predominantly heterosexual. It may take the form of a man marrying another man or a woman tying the knot with a woman. The marriage has a direct bearing on society in terms of health, immorality, thoughts, fantasies, desires, beliefs, attitudes, values, practices, roles, relationships, and a broader realm of human erotic experiences.

The approach to the issues of children is through adoption and artificial reproduction, which violate a fundamental right to be born and raised by their biological mother and father. Indeed, it promotes an assisted-reproduction industry that undermines the connection between biological parents and children, and thereby reconfigures the family.

The gay experience will detach the family from gender, blood, and kinship. Gay families are relatively ungendered, raise children that are biologically unrelated to one or both parents, and often form no more than a shadowy connection between the larger kinship groups. A leading advocate of same-sex marriage, William N. Eskridge, author of *Gaylaw: Challenging Apartheid of the Closet,* writes that building laws upon the gay experience involves the reconfiguration of family, deemphasizing blood, gender, and kinship ties and emphasizing the value of interpersonal commitment.

Logic dictates that same-sex marriage leads to increased access to means of artificial reproduction and surrogate motherhood so that the couples may make up for their biological reality. Such couples will likely press for full access to new assisted reproductive technologies and the right to produce children in whatever way they choose.

Margaret A. Somerville, author of *The Case Against Same-Sex Marriage*, states that marriage involves public recognition of the spouses' relationship and commitment to each other, but that attention is for institutionalizing the procreative relationship to govern the transmission of human life and to protect and promote the wellbeing of the family that results.

In some activities, individual males and females are complete in and of themselves, for example, when they eat, speak, or think. But reproduction requires a man and woman to communicate through a bodily union.

Research has shown that the underlying common cause of homosexuality, whether male or female, is an emotional detachment to the parents of the same sex. The child's masculinity (or femininity) causes insecurity and makes the forming of friendship bonds with those of the same sex much more difficult, frequently leading to painful rejection. Often added to this in the case of boys are mothers who overly compensate, giving the sons too much female affection and fawning over them in the early stages of child development.

A group of physicians presented to the Canadian Parliamentarians scientific evidence that gay marriage is a health risk to Canadians. The report warned that anal sex practiced in gay men has a large number of diseases which are rare or even unknown in the heterosexual population, such as anal cancer, Chlamydia trachomatis, Cryptosporidium, Giardia lamblia, Herpes simplex virus, HIV, Human papillomavirus, Isopoda belli, Microsporidia, Gonorrhea, Syphilis, Hepatitis B and C, and others. Over 70 percent of AIDS diagnoses in gay men (13,019 out of 19,238) age 15 and up to June 2004 were found with these health risk.

The *American Journal of Public Health*, in 2001, in a study group of 3,492 young men who have sex with men, shows the prevalence of HIV infection and high-risk behaviors. The study demonstrates that high-risk behaviors are still quite common among gay men. These references indicate that the passions and acts are unnatural, shameful, and contrary to sound doctrine and the natural use of the body.

Some studies showed that men having sex with other men leads to more significant health risks than men having sex with women, not only because of promiscuity, but also because of the nature of sex among men may cause anal cancer and HIV. All should honor marriage, and the marriage bed kept pure, for God will judge the adulterer and all the sexually immoral (Heb. 13:4).

Timothy and Kathy Keller, authors of *The Meaning of Marriage: Facing the Complexities of Commitment with the Wisdom of God*, sum up how fragmented our understanding of marriage has become. The cultural scene has become so weird that it seems journalists are now required (by some unstated code of ethics) to offer trigger warnings whenever mentioning Christians and marriage in the same sentence. The authors suggest that plenty of people who do not acknowledge God or the Bible, yet who are experiencing happy marriages, are mainly abiding by God's intentions, whether they realize it or not.

God gave his concept of marriage when he said, "Therefore, shall a man leave his father and his mother, and shall cleave unto his wife: and they shall be one flesh. And they were both naked, the man and his wife, and were not ashamed" (Gen. 2:24-25.) God did not say, "A man should leave his father and mother and cleave to another man." God did not say, "A woman should leave her father and mother and cleave to another woman." What can we conclude from this Scripture? God joins the male and female together in marriage and forms a new family. The male leaves the oversight of his parents and cleaves to his wife. It is the same word used to describe Israel's relationship to the Lord: they are to *cling* to Him (Deut. 10:20).

In Matthew 19:5, "For this cause shall a man leave father and mother, and shall cleave to his wife: and they twain shall be one flesh? Jesus gives us two words about the concept of marriage: leave and cleave. The words *leave* and *cleave* are illustrated in the following passage.

Mommy, when your boy gets married, make him leave and cleave to his wife. Break his plate and say, my baby, you are on your own. Fly, fly away and don't you come back until you visit again.

Jesus reaffirms that the only marriage recognized as holy is between a man and a woman. Adam and Eve, not Adam and Bruce. God will never acknowledge that kind of marriage. Gay lobbyists and feminists want homosexuality recognized. It is an unholy union, and an abomination; it will never be known in the court of heaven. They will be denied entrance to the kingdom of God. Thou shalt not lie with humanity, as with womankind: it is an abomination (Lev. 18:22). Do you not know that the unrighteous will not inherit the kingdom of God? Neither gay people nor same sex married people will inherit the kingdom of God (Lev. 18:22).

We also know that the law is made not for the righteous, but for lawbreakers and rebels, the ungodly and sinful, the unholy and irreligious, for those who kill fathers or mothers, murderers, the sexually immoral, those practicing homosexuality, slave traders, liars, perjurers, and for whatever is contrary to the sound doctrine (1 Tim. 1:9–10).

The Bible is very clear from Genesis to Revelation to stay pure as a male and as a female. Ephesians 5:3 says "But fornication, and all uncleanness, or covetousness, let it not be once named among you, as becometh saints." "Let us not be desirous of vain glory, provoking one another, envying one another." Revelation 21:8 tells us, "All of these shall have their part in the lake of fires that burn forever, which is the second death."

What is the principle of covenant marriage? The design is to create a fruitful and multiplying family, which is God's primary purpose of marriage. Same-sex marriage does not serve this purpose. God says there is nothing more holy, nothing more sacred, nothing more precious than a godly mother caring for her children at home. Children are a heritage from the LORD, and offspring are a reward from him (Ps. 127:3). God blesses every one of them.

Philip Travis, a Democrat who opposes same-sex marriage, argued that it could never consummate a marriage. It's physically impossible. We can't get around that marriage requires a union of a man and a woman. A second variation of the argument is like calling a cat a dog. A cat will never be a dog no matter how much you try to call it a dog, or treat it like a dog, or pretend it's a dog. Two people of the same sex cannot "marry" any more than a man can claim the right to "maternity."

Men who dress like women and women who dress like men, God says, "Your purpose is to be a man, and a woman be a woman, and thank God for the difference. Being born is a matter of chance; being born is not a matter of choice. God oversees the selection. The more sophisticated form of the procreation argument is stated this way:

What can man and woman do that man and man can never do? Persons of the same sex can never form a mated pair and be the originators of human reproduction, engage in sexual acts open to new life, have children who are, literally, the embodiment of two-in-one-flesh in a union we call the family.

CHAPTER NINE

A Disaster for the Church

Humanity has defaced the value and honor of covenant marriage and carefully arrived at an understanding of its purpose. But to produce such unaccountable masses of shades and shadows, you thought of some ambitious idea. It will endeavor to demarcate chaos and bewitch some carnally minded humans. We witness much contemplation, and often repeated ponderings, and especially by throwing open the little window towards the entry of the twenty-first century, you will, at last, come to such an idea, however wild, will be altogether unwarranted.

What's most puzzled and confounded will be a long, ugly, obnoxious picture that will drive a godly minded person to tears to think that same-sex marriage is justified and sanctified. It has darted the minds of humans for decades. It's like we are in a midnight gale. It is primordial behavior that is unhealthy, and devilish against the principles of God.

What can the Church say in its proclamation that no one else can say? We must reclaim the mantle and engage in a transformative doctrine that anchors a resurging belief in covenant marriage. A faith that points to God like a road sign that leads to a destination.

God made a woman for a man in marriage. If we are going to continue a faint resemblance of the Creator's desire and avoid His wrath, we must immediately come to our senses. Man's design of marriage has seemed this way: a final theory of my own, partly based upon the aggregated nature of the mind with whom I created.

The opposite idea is contrary to biblical principles, with knots of human idealism and shaped with desire and pleasure. You wondered if this monstrous and savage behavior could ever have such a hacking, horrifying implementation of changing the natural and creating the unnatural, all broken and deformed. The original entered will be blotted out like a restless writer with a pen sojourning through the word of God to remove a hump of morality, justice, truth, and actuality.

Crossing the dusky entry, and on through yonder low-arched ways, and as we attempt to cut through the old precepts of ancient times, that's been great pillars. Humanity didn't need a new breadth of ignorance when we inaugurated same-sex marriage and marriage to things and animals. Humanity has attempted to get rid of the old cockpit and replace it with a new one. Within the shabby instrumentation, the engine cracks, and broken glass canopy, broken wings, it is engulfed in the jaws of swift destruction, but covenant marriage will survive.

The Church may look like an old place with such old, wrinkled planks beneath the floor, shabby shelves, ranged round with faithful people, the message still rings out loudly. Genesis 1:27–28 tells us, "So, God created man in his image, in the image of God he created him; male and female he created them. And God said to them, 'Be fruitful and multiply and fill the earth and subdue it and have dominion over the fish of the sea and the birds of the heavens and over every living thing that moves on the earth" (Gen. 2:24). "Heaven and earth will pass away, but my words will never pass away" (Matt. 24:35). It is imperative that the Church establish a strong, definitive position against same-sex marriage.

Humanity has lost contact with God and has begun to operate within the fellowship of its senses. Men who are ruled by their minds cannot know God, see Him, have fellowship with Him, or understand His revelation. Humanity then develops a railing against the faith in Christ, and it does not affect them.

The Church is failing in its duty to a faltering culture. The Church is like iron rods that hold the concrete of covenant marriage together but has become like motorists who drive over the highway every day with little thoughts of the iron rods beneath the concrete surface. These rods provide the connection and enable the concrete to remain intact and withstand the constant pressure of the ongoing traffic. What has the Church done to change the minds of men operating in their devilish senses? The duty of the Church is to provide the congregation with a spiritual diet that nourishes both the mind and the soul and helps to weather the advancement.

The Church continues to face stiff opposition from outside forces. The evil of same-sex marriage is just outside the door of the Church, knocking to force itself into the synagogue. Some churches have failed to give logical, analytical, and investigative reasons that challenge these external forces. Therefore, it has locked the doors to keep out the concept, but the world is knocking on the doors. In recent years, the Church has been held under scrutiny and offers no answers towards the problem of same-sex marriage.

A covenant marriage is between a man and a woman, and a man should have his wife and each woman her husband (Gen. 2:24). Scriptures do not support any other way of marriage. These issues have become ubiquitous in the Church, and the body of Christ must join the fight against the abomination. The Church has failed to respond because of stiff opposition from outside forces like freedom of choice, laws, and atheist views. One decade, the Church is buying buses, picking up hundreds of children in the neighborhood for Bible camps, and starting twelve-step support groups. Another decade, the Church has seeker-sensitive worship churches. The Church must give logical and analytical reasons against the practice of same-sex marriage. The paramount concern is to help society return to God's plan for marriage. It's not going to be easy.

The responsibility of the Church toward marriage is to teach and unveil the shadows cast upon the foundation of marriage in a culture that now recognizes marriage in ways currently active that are not biblical.

- The Church is no longer relevant to what we know.

- The Church did not address the sexual revolution with the knowledge to withstand the pressures of the world.

- The Church remained ignorant and silent against same-sex marriage and needs to do something else.

- The Church has not translated the New Testament message to address contemporary problems.

- Churches do not have programs for the reconciliation, rebuilding, and forgiveness for those in the Church and those who choose to return.

- The world is in an endless cycle of social fast lanes and sinfulness. The Church is losing its influence, and the world is influencing the Church in worldly affairs.

The present generation and society are in trouble. The argument or excuse used against the Church is an individual choice. The government guarantees individual inalienable rights, but in its fullest essence, has caused decay. The Church has become biased against a challenging problem. The typical reaction to marriage was once a high trust in God blessing the union. However, Christianity is fading rapidly among Christians, and now we are becoming integrated into the ways of the world.

The greatest challenge to the Church will continue to be same-sex marriage. Jesus taught, "And when these things begin to take place, stand up and lift your heads because your redemption is drawing near" (Lk. 21:28). Let us pray with purpose and act in faith. Some other challenges the Church will face in the twenty-first century never dreamed possible include:

1. The Church will meet an older generation by 2030. The Church will have an impossible task of blending together the four generational groups found in churches: builders (born before 1945), boomers (1945–64), busters and Gen x (1965–1983), and bringers/millennials (born since1984). Discontent over worship styles and music. The Church must address the needs of all people God places in its care regardless of age or gender (2 Cor. 12:20–21).

2. There will be significant attempts to silence the gifts of the Spirit in public meetings and to further compromise teachings (1 Cor. 14:37–39).

3. The corporate world will adopt unscriptural tactics into religious procedures (2 Tim. 3:5).

4. America will decline as the dominant influence in the world. The only hope is a return of God's glory, by again placing total trust in God (Heb. 4:12).

5. The Church will lose respect in the community. Godly values and concepts will be relegated to fables, myths, and legends (1 Tim. 2:1,2).

6. Individuals who desire selfish control over the Church will undermine the leaders and seek to cause divisions

over petty and insignificant issues to destroy harmony and conventional wisdom and Scripture teachings (Jer. 3:15).

7. The core value of the American family will continue to disintegrate (Eph. 5:21–33).

8. Throughout America, the distortion of the truth will intensify. Lies will saturate every institution of the nation (Jn. 14:16–18).

9. The cities of America (large and small) will continue to serve as havens for crime, violence, perversion, and drugs. The Church must aggressively reach out with evangelism, food, clothing, physical labor, counsel, and genuine love (Lk. 10:1–12).

10. The world will direct hostility toward the Church with open persecution to followers. The Gospel message will permeate the media, government, medical, and research organizations, the entertainment industry, and educational institutions with a loud shout (1 Cor. 4:10–12).

11. America will continue to become multi-cultural, international, and racially/sexually diverse. We need to model godly behavior in our homes, schools, congregations, and communities (2 Cor. 4:1–6).

12. The economic crisis in the world will worsen, as the Bible predicted (Mal. 3:10–12).

The Church must adopt some innovative approaches to escape from becoming a victim of conditioning and fight against political agendas to enter and lead it away from its purpose. The laws signed by President Obama are evidence of this conditioning dichotomy toward the subject of same-sex marriage. The current issues for the Church are different than those of previous generations. Constitutional laws affecting worship in public places have created pressures and challenges against religious freedom. These laws have weakened religious rights and have become proficient in the ways of the world. The Church must become knowledgeable about these changes and meet the challenges. Same-sex marriage is a disaster for the Church.

Satan is creating lies, and they are becoming footstools in the world. "Neither give place to the devil" (Eph. 4:27). When we realize that Satan governs the carnal mind, it is easy to understand how man develops a system of knowledge without one's being conscious of it. It is enmity against God. The intention of such men cannot know God. God needs to dominate our thoughts. The current generations, Generation X, Y, and Z have impacted organizational structure, workplace communications, employee training, and the faith once held by their parents and grandparents.

Same-sex marriage has already created different mindsets between millennials and Generation Z. The Church has failed to challenge them to an understanding of the biblical expectations that should emerge from these generations. The workplace is having a more significant influence on the faith of the younger generation in many ways, without biblical expectations.

1. Realistic vs. Optimistic. Seventy-seven percent of Generation Z expect to work harder than previous generations.

2. Digital Natives vs. Digital Pioneers. Forty percent of Generation Z said that working Wi-Fi was more important to them than working bathrooms.

3. Private vs. Public. Seventy percent of Generation Z would rather share personal information with their pet than with their boss.

4. On-Demand Learning vs. Formally Educated. Seventy-five percent of Generation Z say there are other ways of getting a good education than going to college.

5. Global Citizen vs. Global Spectator. Fifty-eight percent of adults worldwide ages 35+ agree that "kids today have more in common with their global peers than they do with adults in their country."

The Church is not mentioned as influencing or changing the minds of Generation Z presently, because they have fewer concerns with their faith. Here are some encouraging findings from more than eight hundred millennials across the United States.

1. It's a spiritual world.

2. Twenty percent believe Satan is merely a symbol of evil.

3. Twenty percent believe being good gets you to Heaven.

4. Fifty to eighty percent feel Christian faith is essential.

5. Sixty-one to eighty percent feel Christianity can meet their spiritual needs.

Christianity in the United States is waning. The rates of church attendance, religious affiliation, belief in God, prayer, and Bible-reading have been dropping for decades. Americans' views are becoming more post-Christian and, concurrently, religious identity is changing. Generation Z: Born between 1999 and 2015, they are the first truly "post-Christian" generation. More than any other generation before them, Gen Z does not assert a religious identity.

The decline in church attendance is more about values. Going to church must add clarity to the young people's lives. How we connect with millennials in the twenty-first century is critical. Sixty-five to ninety-five percent share e-mail, cell numbers, or social media. They desire conversation about spiritual matters and believe that

Jesus may have answers for them. But they are overwhelmed, distracted, exhausted, and mistrusting. Finding faith must be on their terms, and many are attracted to new ideas.

In the twenty-first century, the membership of some churches is declining. But what most puzzles and stuns is something hovering in the center of a picture over a dim, perpendicular line floating in a nameless sea. There is a sort of indefinite, half-attained, unimaginable thoughts that is involuntarily and less marvelous about the approach. Man is now living in the realm of his senses and desires. It may manifest itself in a physical act that directs and is in more control than the spiritual.

The Church is in a disaster in contemporary times and may be compare to a ship surviving a great hurricane; the half-floundered ship weltering there with its dismantled masts alone visible; and in an exasperated position, the craft is seen as a relic from the past. Jesus said to Peter, "And I say also unto thee, that thou art Peter, and upon this rock I will build my church; and the gates of hell shall not prevail against it" (Matt. 16:18). Same-sex marriage is gaining control of covenant marriage.

Same-sex marriage is having a tremendous impact on church policies and membership.

Humanity does not have the right to make its laws, which God has ordained to obey. A.T. Robertson, a Baptist scholar, argued that the "mind of the flesh" does not possess the ability "to receive the things of the Spirit." The initiative comes from God, whose Holy Spirit makes it possible.

The word *dunamis* comes from a Greek word, which means "strength, power, or ability to the Church. The English word implies dynamite, dynamo, and dynamic. It's not just any power. Some testimonies of the Church's power are reported in the Bible.

The angel answered, "And the angel came in unto her, and said, Hail, thou that art highly favor, the Lord is with thee: blessed art thou among women." (Luke 1:28).

But ye shall receive power, after that the Holy Ghost is come upon you: and ye shall be witnesses unto me both in Jerusalem, and in all Judaea, and in Samaria, and unto the uttermost part of the earth. (Acts 1:8).

But we have this treasure in earthen vessels, that the excellency of the power may be of God, and not of us. (2 Cor. 4:7).

For God hath not given us the spirit of fear; but of power, and of love, and of a sound mind. (2 Tim. 1:7).

Now unto him that is able to do exceedingly abundantly above all that we ask or think, according to the power that worketh in us, unto him be glory in the church by Christ Jesus throughout all ages, world without end. Amen. (Eph. 3:20–21).

With the power (dunamis) through Jesus, the apostles continued to testify of the resurrection of Jesus Christ, and great favors were upon them. The Church can be rekindled and use its power to bring about transformation of covenant marriage back to society (Acts 4:33). Dunamis, through the power of God, gives the Church the miraculous power to deal with diseases. Dunamis provides the Church with the supernatural power to deal with demons. It provides the Church with the miraculous power to deal with circumstances. It gives the Church miraculous power to overturn the laws passed for same-sex marriage. The Church, with its strength, power, and ability, needs to meet evil forces that are destroying humanity and cease the wrath of God to come.

The Church is equipped with the power and authority to conquer and destroy the challenge of humanity with power from God. The Church also can restore hope, joy, and peace to a sin-sick world.

The Church has the power, purpose, and a calling. The Church must confess what we are in Christ. We must admit that by His stripes, the world can be healed of infirmities.

"But ye are a chosen generation, a royal priesthood, a holy nation, a peculiar people; that ye should shew forth the praises of him who hath called you out of darkness into his marvelous light. Which in time past were not a people but are now the people of God: which had not obtained mercy, but now have obtained mercy" (1 Pet. 2:9–10). "And we know that all things work together for good to them that love God, to them who are the called according to his purpose" (Rom. 8:28).

The U.S. Supreme Court's legalization of gay marriage in America in 2015 created changes to Church policy, including several that seek to lift longstanding bans and grant the same privileges as covenant marriage. Churches are now faced with two significant challenges. First, the Church needs to assess how it can improve and diminish the influence of sexuality to a level that prevents God from taking drastic actions against the nation and present generations. Secondly, the Church must be prepared to provide proper biblical counsel to those within same-sex unions who want to escape the lifestyle and come to Christ.

Dave and Ann Wilson, authors of the book *Vertical Marriage*, tell us, "The secret of getting the marriage we are looking for: the horizontal marriage relationship just doesn't work until the vertical relationship with Christ is first." The Church must see this in Scripture as complete with the need to extend themselves to make the message of godly marriage relevant to a changing world. Does this mean that the Church needs to step forward? Yes, the Church must continue to have clear boundaries, and Christians must guard these boundaries. Some people are beleaguered and disoriented in their beliefs and need to be navigated back on course.

The careful inquiries and enforcement of individual rights are rational and have arrived at an understanding of the ambitious endeavor. Such unaccountable masses of people have generated chaos and bewitched the world with their beliefs about same-sex marriage. The saints of God need to keep a door open towards the front of the church entry and welcome those back into the flock who repent and give up same-sex marriage.

However wild and altogether unwarranted and unchristian, the Church is conforming to the world. On the contrary, the Church and Christians are supposed to transform the world, turning people from worldly desires and renewing their minds to God's perfection as possible. Same-sex marriage is unacceptable and is creating a disaster for the Church. Young minds in the twenty-first century are being shaped by music, media, internet, cell phones, culture, and peer pressure. Millennials born 1981–1996 (22–37 years old now) and post-millennials born 1997–present (0–21 years old) agree that same-sex marriage is a new sexual revolution. Many have been caught up in a web of seekers. The percentage in support of same-sex marriage has climbed from 53 in 2007 to 70 percent last year. Now, for the first time, more than 56 percent of baby boomers born 1946–1964 (54–72 years old) favor allowing same-sex marriage. Support for same-sex marriage has grown among the silent generation born 1928–1945 (73–90 years old) at 41 percent. Two-thirds of Catholics now support same-sex marriage, as do a similar share of white mainline Protestants, at 68 percent. The United Methodist Church voted recently to strengthen its ban on gay and lesbian clergy and same-sex marriages, a decision that could split the nation's second-largest Protestant church. The resolution passed in a 53 percent to 47 percent vote and is the latest eruption in the fight over the future of human sexuality as Christians.

Paul warned, "Preach the word; be instant in season, out of season; reprove, rebuke, exhort with all longsuffering and doctrine. For the time will come when they will not endure sound doctrine; but after their own lusts shall they heap to themselves teachers, having itching ears; and they shall turn away their ears from the truth, and shall be turned unto fables" (2 Tim. 4:2-4). God condemns same-sex marriage.

In 1973, David Kinnaman wrote a book entitled *Unchristian: What a new generation thinks about Christianity and why it matters*, which is based on research on the unchristian. The book reflects outsiders' most common reaction to the faith. They believe that Christians no longer represent what Jesus had in mind, and the unchristian does not attend church. Many of the older church members are dying out, and there is a difference in the spirituality of today's church. Humanity has attempted to kill the Spirit of God in covenant marriage. Marriage is compared to a beautiful temple which is dedicated to God, but now it is dedicated to men as a showcase of pride. "Pride goes before destruction, and a haughty spirit before a fall" (Prov. 16:18).

The Church exists to save lost souls destined for hell; not to bless the means of their damnation. The Church has no power to sanction marriage outside of the plan of God. No matter what the government may legislate, the law of God is clear. Same-sex marriage is not a godly marriage if it is a same-sex union. F. Yeakley's book entitled *Why They Left: Listening to Those Who Have Left Churches of Christ* states, "The Church must be willing to reverse the current trends of decline and perform some self-reflection."

The ancient text offers the finest of biblical advice for contemporary times and underscores the need for teaching each generation about covenant marriage. God is always concerned for the welfare of each generation. It is imperative that the previous generations serve as a consistent role model for the next generation and for outsiders. Prior generations cannot just preach to the future generations and expect them to follow the rules. The present generations need to see the previous generations admitting mistakes and learn from those mistakes. It is the responsibility of the Church to lead every generation to where God wants them to be. Every effort must be made to reach and foster principles to lead them in the right direction.

We look at couples of same-sex marriages knocking on the church doors wanting to come in to tear the church apart to reflect upon some privileges. They want to go to church and enjoy the same cushioned pews you enjoy, the same air-conditioning, the same lights, enjoy the same choir singing, hear the same sermons, give an offering, and sneak out of the church and won't give their full life to Christ. They are all spiritual shoplifters.

The Church must continue to resist the pressure of same-sex marriage, and to animals and things.

1. Some worshippers have become sophisticated and educated in individual rights.

2. Excessive pride has permitted some worshippers to uphold the Church constitution for those of same-sex marriage.

3. Personal desires have superseded godly principles of covenant marriage.

4. The Church should never lose its vision of covenant marriage and God's expectations of marriage.

The congregation should not look back each time the church doors open to see who's coming into the service unless it is for security reasons. If a church is teaching and preaching the principles of God, those with the wrong intents and practices will not survive. "The Spirit of the Lord is upon me, because he hath anointed me to preach the gospel to the poor; he hath sent me to heal the brokenhearted, to preach deliverance to the captives, and recovering of sight to the blind, to set at liberty them that are bruised, to preach the acceptable year of the Lord" (Lk. 4:18–19). He has sent the Son to heal, to offer liberty to the bruised, and to teach the accepted messages of the Lord.

History has shown that humanity tends to veer off in the wrong direction. The problem is how the churches, led by preachers, elders, and deacons, and supported by a host of auxiliaries, can lead them back. How can we overcome this unfortunate dilemma of same-sex marriage? How can this disaster end? The enemy's most popular weapons he uses against you are worry, anxiety, and fear. These life forces can overwhelm you with a thick shadow of darkness, controlling your every move and decision-making.

For God hath not given us the spirit of fear; but of power, and love, and a sound mind (2 Tim. 1:7).

Fear thou not; for I am with thee be not dismayed; for I am thy God: I will strengthen thee; yea, I will help thee; yea, I will uphold thee with the right hand of my righteousness (Isa. 41:10).

The Church's mission is to give godly counsel to every generation, which includes covenant marriage. It has and will always have the responsibility to communicate to the people how to apply God's truth to their lives. If the Church fails to carry out its mission, demonstrating faithfully those things that would benefit every generation, it will certainly perish. A connection can develop when the Church starts to minister directly in various avenues, using unified prayers against same-sex marriage.

However, it may seem as if the Church is fading into a helpless institution lacking the power it once obtained. The messages of God's historical application of covenant marriage in the twenty-first century has not lost its supremacy. Humanity needs to carefully exam history and regain some essential lessons that God is in charge, and He will always oversee every aspect of marriage.

A better day is coming, a day when King Jesus will vacuum off the wicked, and the faithful will be the only ones left. The righteous do not fight for their rights, do not insist upon personal justification, and do not always have to correct others. We do not return insult for insult and use force to intimidate, but we know the battle is the Lord's. Christians are those loved by God; sinners who have fallen but were helped to stand again, and even still some are unsteady in their marriage and often fall short of the glory of God because of their unfaithfulness. There is hope that church people will act like Christ, and sometimes they do. Especially as the love of Christ shines through them like a diamond to light. It affects your relationship with your family, your friends, and God. Your faith will determine your success and failures, physical and spiritual.

The Church is a blessed institution. Covenant marriage is a valuable institution of humanity and the Church still has the responsibility to correct humanity. We have the power to work within and accomplish the will of God in marriage and glorify Christ Jesus. The Church is His bride. Christians must develop a spiritual appetite for covenant marriage. The Church is a blessed institution and has the power at work within to accomplish abundantly far more than it can imagine, to him be glory in Christ Jesus to all generations, forever and ever.

CHAPTER TEN

Making Your Marriage Work

Marriage is a continual, ongoing pursuit to keep your relationship intact. The foremost passionate aspiration is a personal walk that lasts to the end of your life. The ingredients that make marriage work are God-centered; the unconditional love, a healthy communication, trust and honesty, laughter, compatibility, commitment, security, respect, room for growth to bring out the best for the union, and the blessings of God's enabling grace.

Covenant marriage should be a daily relationship fitness workout, like physical fitness. It must not cease to remain an achieving goal for life after you have secured and tied the knot. We work for the better and eliminate the worst, even though we anticipate the best.

Every marriage is going to have some ups and downs. Some problems of marriage include fears of the unknown, divorce, unfaithfulness, falling out of love; niggling, and nagging. Resentment will start to build. The relationship needs a kind of trust, safety, security, commitment, and spiritual intimacy to keep the marriage thriving when you manage the matters of marriage. To get there, you can share Scriptures about a covenant marriage relationship and talk about the problems using the techniques of communication.

When you listen to sports players talk after they win championships, someone will always say, we closed ranks against all opposition. The greatest enemy is you against the world. A successful marriage works the same way.

In our culture today, the view of faults is in the other person. You often feel that no flaws are in you. But you say to your partner, you get on my last nerve. Your boss is at fault. You have a right to steal from him or cheat him. God is at fault. He made you this way. You have a right to act this way because he made you with a temper, anger, and a lustful desire.

Webster's dictionary defines the word *wholehearted* as marked by a complete sincere commitment that was once recognized as an incredible value in a relationship. Paul speaks of an awareness that values the importance of uniqueness that allows you to remain in a loving relationship with another whose personal qualities and habits differ from your own. Patience, kindness, endurance, and sympathy are positive qualities relative to the critical nature of the relationship. The expression of love is intended to the other in all his or her fullness, even at the cost of self.

In marriage, this expression of love draws partners together rather than apart in ways that result in a continuous and renewed appreciation of the other's way of being and doing. Love must be sincere. Hate what is evil; cling to what is right. Be devoted to one another in love and honor one another above yourselves. Never be lacking in zeal, but keep your spiritual fervor, serving the Lord. Be joyful in hope, patient in afflictions, and faithful in prayer (Rom. 12:9–12). Love each other in the same way you want to be loved. There is no greater love (John 15:12-13).

Rather than turning personal preferences into a battlefield, love places things in perspective. Love moves persons toward considering and communicating together about the ideal images that you have and your way of doing things, revising them in ways that advance the marriage toward a shared mutual relationship. Tina Turner raised a question in her recording "What's Love Got to Do with It?" Love enriches, edifies, and endures. You speak with the tongues of men and of angels and have not love, you become as sounding brass, or a tinkling cymbal. You may have the gift of prophecy and understand all mysteries, and all knowledge and have the faith to remove mountains, and have not love your spouse, you are nothing. You may bestow all your goods to feed the poor, and though you give your body as a sacrifice to serving humanity, and have not love your spouse, it profits you nothing. Love suffer long and is kind. It does not envy, vaunt itself, or puffed up. Love do not behave itself unseemly, seek no evil against your spouse. Love rejoice not in iniquity but in the truth. Love bears all things, believe, hope, and endure all things in your marriage (1 Cor. 13:7).

Smiley Blanton's book entitled *Love or Perish* said:

Without love, hopes will perish.

Without love, your dreams, and creativity perish.

Without love, your families, and churches perish.

Without love, friendship perish.

Without love, the intimacies of romance perish.

Without love, the desire to go on living can perish.

Love detects needs and does what is best for the other person without being told. It must bring us to the point of seeing and acting on a marital relationship as a sacred action. Five words, "I will love you always," can improve your marriage. As we grow older, you say them less and show less actions. You made promises to love your spouse forever. It is a good idea to say them as often as possible. It may be a chilly, stormy day; it can be refreshing to say to your spouse, "I do love you."

Love is patient and kind; love does not envy or boast; it is not arrogant or rude. It does not insist on its own way; it is not irritable or resentful. Love does not rejoice at wrongdoing but rejoices with the truth. Love bears all things, believes all things, hopes all things, endures all things (1 Cor. 13:4–7).

Marriage is a sacred relationship in God's eyes, and it stands to reason that prayer is needed in a marriage relationship. Pray together on a regular plan for your marriage success. Father Patrick Peyton and the Roman Catholic Family Rosary Crusade tells us, "There is power in prayer. A family that prays together stays together." Prayer is key to any successful marriage. God must be the head of any union that is expected to last. Here are some Scriptures to consider.

1. Lord may the delight be in you, and the marriage meditate on your laws, day and night. "For I know the plans I have for you," declares the Lord, "plans to prosper you and not to harm you, plans to give you hope and a future (Jer. 29:11).

2. When you do so, your marriage and your family will be like a tree planted by streams of water, which yields fruit in its season and whose leaf does not wither will prosper day and night (Ps. 1:1–3).

3. Lord, make the marriage strong for you. The wisdom of marriage comes from the Lord.

4. "Be completely humble and gentle; be patient, bearing with one another in love. Make every effort to keep the unity of the Spirit through the bond of peace" (Eph. 4:2-3).

5. Give the couple humble hearts toward one another, not looking to personal interests, but the interests of your spouse. "Let this mind be in you, which was also in Christ Jesus" (Phil. 2:5).

6. May this marriage rejoice and rest in the knowledge that you give as your children (Isa. 62:5).

Share your spiritual ministry in serving the Lord together. Christ prayed for oneness in the relationship. He emphasized the purpose of oneness in our ministry and marriage, so the world believes in your ministry. You can minister to your families, neighbors, friends, looking beyond yourselves to minister to others.

So many people have come from broken homes, and when problems and disappointments occur in their life, they blame them on their parents. Denials, lies, and illusions have twisted minds and created scenarios of fantasies harmful to the marriage. You want more out of life. You wake up one day and feel like you are in the worst situation of your life, and your marriage has become boring. Satan will convince you to break away from your moral obligation. The first attack will be to convince you that when things go astray, it's somebody's fault. You're not happy anymore, and you have the right to get even with your spouse. Your wife is at fault.

It takes a commitment to combine two minds with different physical and spiritual attributes into one sustained relationship. Therefore, before the connection, the wife and husband should know their duties. The best warranty of your marriage is how you show each other how much you love the union, and then the world will see how much it means to you. Marriage needs nurturing like you enjoy the best meal of all times. An old proverb suggests that you are what you eat. Marriage is what you nurture it to be.

What is a good marriage? The answer depends on looking at it from a secular or religious perspective. Those seeking the secular view would say that a good marriage is made up of love, trust, honesty, and practical understanding between the spouses. Christians look at the religious perspective of a covenant marriage, which includes love, respect, trust, reliability, and God's aspect of marriage.

Wilson Yates's essay, *The Protestant View of Marriage*, outlines six characteristics of marriage commitment that are illustrated in a covenant. The first is the duty of the spouses to create a life of intimate relationship rooted in love, intimacy, romance, and emotion for life-long companionship. The second characteristic is building honesty, trust, and openness in a life of intimate fellowship. Develop honesty and trust by telling the truth. The third element of the covenant marriage is the "commitment to explore and respond to community responsibilities of Christian faith in Jesus." The fourth aspect is upholding all aspects of the covenant, such as love and order. The fifth quality of engagement is a determination to create limitations and rules of behavior in the relationship both spouses can agree and share. Lastly, the sixth element has to do with fixing the difficulties in the marriage with the possibilities of seeking help before you try divorce.

I believe there are differences between religious and secular interpretations. But when it comes to marriage, each has something in common when it comes to the conditions of a good marriage. Those who believe in the religious perspective think that marriage is a commitment between two individuals in an intimate relationship who promise to care for each other's human needs for life. Covenant marriage teaches about God. Covenant marriage is modeled after the marriage of Christ and the Church. Those who believe in the secular perspective accept marriage as a commitment between the same sex, with animals, or something else to develop intimate relationships to care for the other human needs. In a secular marriage, that is impossible (children).

Many marriages begin singing a familiar song, "I Will Love You Always." They soon find themselves downloading the tune, "Love Has Lost Its Fire." You are saying to yourself, "There is more to marriage then what I expected." The old ship of matrimony has sailed into some troubled seas, and some couples are jumping overboard by the thousands. Many will stay chained to the mast for the children, business, avoid social pressure, even the Church, but they have stopped enjoying the trip. A good marriage is one intended for life on the faithful fellowship train until death. It's going to take two to achieve this endeavor, the wife and the loving leadership of a husband.

Never underestimate problems in marriage or the power to cope with it. In any marriage, you are going to have questions. That is the reality of marriage. Realize that you will have issues, but you can solve them by facing them daily. Your reaction to any problem will have a lot to do with the outcome.

I have seen people face catastrophe with a negative attitude. They turned their problems into a disaster. They turned their marriage upside down because they didn't want to compromise. Some couples must face the issues and tell themselves the problem is too big for us to tackle. We need to shrink it down to size, realize that we need help in finding solutions and realistic ways to do what is necessary to keep us together. Norman Vincent Peale asserted, "Positive thinking is how you think about a problem. Enthusiasm is how you feel about the problem and determination is what you do about the problem." If you want to solve your problems in marriage, you can seek help. The key to problem-solving is to approach the problem in the right way.

Don't let your marriage become abusive. The first argument is led by a frustrated husband who may misuse his spouse by justifying his autonomous attitudes, behavior, and actions. The man who misappropriates his spouse will focus on his freedom. He will defend his actions in doing whatever he pleases without consulting with his spouse or having no care for what she thinks. A husband can be abusive if he does not listen to the desires of his wife. If the marriage is going to work, again I say, the husband and wife must understand their duties. Ephesians 5:23 tells us, "For the husband is the head of the wife." But that does not mean the man is smarter than the woman. Both are of infinite worth, made in the image of God, and highly intelligent creatures. It does not mean the husband is a dictator. Can you imagine God planning without informing the Son? There is complete communication and absolute unity in every decision. Many wives shudder when they hear this Scripture. Neither the husband nor the wife has complete authority in the marriage. Ephesians 5:22 tells us, "Submitting yourselves one to another in the fear of God."

Anne E. Streaty Wimberly, director of Youth Hope-Builders Academy and Professor Emerita of Christian Education, Interdenominational Theological Center, Atlanta, Georgia, invites couples to engage in "*Get the Rap on Marital Relationships.*"

Put the "R" in Rap.

Recall the vows you made at your wedding.

Review your vows.

Reaffirm your vows.

Put the "A" in Rap (Activate a spiritually

life).

Assess the importance of love in your marriage to other goals within and outside of marriage. Include your assessment of the impact of media on your views of marriage, considering your understanding of love at the center of marriage and a godly life. Anchor yourselves in the wisdom of the Christian faith through your study of Paul's message in 1 Corinthians 13:4–8 and participate in marriage enrichment seminars. Activate a spiritually rich marital ritual life of individuals, shared Bible study; pray for power to manage the outside pressures and cultivate a nurturing, loving relationship characterized by open communication, honesty, mutuality, cooperation, reliability, and generosity. William Barclay comments on Paul's emphasis on the absolute completeness of love that is seen in God's love through Christ that provides a model for loving relationships.

Cindy and Steve Wright express that Paul points out that love in marital relationships is immeasurable, extravagant, and reflects the love of God that when others see how you treat each other, they want to know your secret because they will want a marriage as healthy as yours.

Honor your marriage. It's, not a recommendation, it is a principle. If I give you a suggestion that means you have a choice to obey or disobey. If God gives you a commandment, you have no choice but to obey.

- The first commandment tells us, "Thy shall have no other gods before me" (Exod. 20:3). God wants an exclusive relationship with Him in your marriage. Henry Ford was asked on his 50th wedding anniversary what his secret to a successful marriage was. He said, "The secret to my successful marriage is the same secret I have in business. I stick to the same model." No competition should exist in marriage. One God. One man. One woman until death do you part. Romans 7:2 says, "For the woman which hath an husband is bound by the law to her husband so long as he lives; but if the husband be dead, she is loosed from the law of her husband." First Corinthians 7:39, says, "The wife is bound by the law as long as her husband lives; but if her husband be dead, she is at liberty to be married to whom she will; only in the Lord."

- The second commandment: Love God and don't love a substitute. Exodus 20:4–6 gives the principle for a healthy marriage: We do not serve any idols. A wife or husband is a real-life partner, and they shouldn't be looking for excitement in things such as pornography, same-sex partner, or any other that will replace the wife in a sexual relationship.

- The third commandment is to speak caring words about your partner. Exodus 20:7 says, "Thou shalt not take the name of the LORD thy God in vain; for the LORD will not hold him guiltless that taketh his name in vain." Harsh and unkind words can damage a marriage in negative ways. Kind words can fill a heart with love, joy, peace, and happiness, or they can create hate and bitterness.

- The fourth commandment is to spend quality time alone together. God orders us to keep the Sabbath holy (Exod. 20:8). Sabbath means intermission—to lay down your work and to rest. God asks for time with Him in a long-term relationship. A husband and wife need scheduled time together for their marriage to flourish and keep it holy.

- The fifth commandment is to honor your partner by showing him/her how grateful you are for each other. Exodus 20:12 tells us, "Honor thy father and thy mother: that thy days may be long upon the land which the LORD thy God giveth thee." That means to invest time, effort and money in your families and show appreciation for them.

- The sixth commandment is don't destroy your partner but be soft and sweet. Exodus 20:13 orders us not to commit murder. Some people may say, I haven't thought about divorce, but murder? I think about that often! Violence, abuse, short tempers destroy a marriage relationship and self-image if both partners use these strategies. They can lead to murder.

- The seventh commandment tells us, "Do not commit adultery" (Exod. 20:14). An affair is one of the most destructive things that can happen in a marriage. We need to beware of affairs that are committed by our thoughts and can lead to adultery, which is the most serious sin in marriage. Mathew 5:28 says: "But I say unto you, that whosoever looks on a woman to lust after her hath committed adultery with her already in his heart." There is no place for lust in marriage. Love gives, lust takes. Love serves, lust claims. Love feeds, lust throttles. The marriage bed should be kept pure, for God will judge the adulterer and all the sexually immoral. (Heb. 13:4). Sex is a holy institution and may be enjoyed within the boundaries and holiness of marriage.

- The eighth commandment is to be a person of integrity. Exodus 20:15 advises us not to steal. The person you marry should be a person of integrity. Someone you respect, trust, and adore to be in the relationship with. Don't let someone steal love for your spouse.

- The ninth commandment is to be truthful. Exodus 20:16 says, you shall not bear false witness against your neighbor, your partner, or anything for whatever reasons. Then you will know the truth, and the truth will set you free (Jn. 8:32). Honesty and trust are at the heart of a good marriage.

- The tenth commandment is to be satisfied with what you have. Exodus 20:17 says, "Thou shalt not bear false witness against thy neighbor. You may not covet. Receive your blessings from the Lord with thanksgiving, which includes the uniqueness of your spouse. Don't think the grass is greener on the other side of the fence; that will get you into troubled waters.

If your covenant marriage is going to work, don't get to the point and say, "It's too late." Miracles do happen, and you need to believe that Jesus has the preventive medicine. Maybe you need a single breakthrough. He seeks your attention. If you are willing to work at it, it can become a reality. You can imagine what it would be like to have a degree of perfection in your marriage. If you cannot imagine growth, revaluate your intention to marry. Recognize your weaknesses and initiate your plan of improvement and start working.

CHAPTER ELEVEN

Blessed Are Those Who Marry

Most marriages today prepare for a short-term journey with a first-degree assault filled with malicious intentions of turning sour. The traditional marriage structure is in jeopardy when we alter the plan of God for marriage. The husband is recognized as king, priest, and prophet in the home. He is a leader and lover of the family. He listens, prays, blesses, and guides his family. The mother, wife, queen, is the helpmate for him to meet his every need.

The truth about marriage today is captivated by contemporary ideals of marriage rather than the traditional standards of a covenant marriage. Those who walk in the Spirit with their marriage are blessed. "Walk in the Spirit, and ye shall not fulfil the lust of the flesh" (Gal. 5:16).

The attitude of marriage started long before you accepted your vows. It started when you began to select a mate. Christian marriage is a solemn and public covenant between a man and a woman in the presence of God. But covenant marriage needs to return to the principles of God desperately. The institution of marriage first was ordained by God before the law, civilization, government, and a system of worship (the Church) was structured. It is the primary institution originated by Almighty God. Jesus said, "What God has created, it is unwise to create a new proposal, design, and strategy. Humanity has made a turn at the crossroad and comes to envision a way better than God's ways.

Many factors are influencing the demise of marriage today. The mention of same-sex marriage was just one of many factors that I believe grieve God's heart and compromise the family. As you may know, I uphold traditional biblical truths that the sanctity of marriage is between a man and a woman.

Marriage is a new journey, and many are trying to make it condescend to a corrupt level of conduct and course to prepare another way to specific heights, individual levels, and defined goals. They do not care about God's penalty. They do not care about the drawbacks, their mild-mannered, dispositional trifling conduct and demeanor that is not of God.

Marriages face lots of issues: Earning money, how to handle our money, how to share the bills, where to buy a home, how to buy a house, furnishing an apartment, maintaining a house, dividing chores around the house, cooking nightly dinners, accumulating things, how to pay for things, paying off debt, thinking about having children, deciding when to have children, birth control issues, fertility issues, saving for college educations for children, paying off school loans, saving for retirement, insurance decisions, where the children attend school, how to pay for private schools, building social lives, separating from old friends, making new friends, exercising, health, stress, sex, entertainment, death of parents, babysitting, budget, overspending, furthering education, choosing doctors, changing or losing jobs, mental health, work, travel, pet issues, child extracurricular activities, not enough time in a day, childrearing conflict, disciplining children, finding time for everything, whether to work or be at home, personal issues, family, the in-laws, blending families, spending too much time at work, snoring, bad habits, mixing friends and social circles, learning to compromise, aging, substance abuse, relationship issues, which church to attend, vacation planning, estate planning, and burial planning. Wow!

The Church in this present generation must keep a spirit of revival in covenant marriage. Keep the door open for generations to teach the biblical precepts about marriage. God is going to place His wrath on those who alter his plan, and I believe it is going to be soon. Marriage is an institution that belongs to God and not man.

We must confess that we do foolish things sometimes. I drove my automobile off the road and got stuck in the mud. At that point, I got out of the car and scrounged around for a board and tried to dig myself out. Next, I found a piece of wood and put that underneath the tires. By this time, I'm going down, down, down. I am stuck in the mud! Well, I want someone to come and pull me out. I need your help. Lord, I'm helpless here. Lord, get me out. A man came and said, "Are you stuck?" I replied, "Obviously, I am." He said, "Well, I have a cable in my car." We hooked up my car to his truck, and he pulled me slowly out of the mud. When I got back on solid ground, I was so grateful that he had come along. I do believe God sent me someone in a four-wheel truck with a cable. He advised me, "Now, you be careful," then he was on his way.

Many couples are stuck in the mud and sinking deeper and deeper. They say, "I can get myself out. I can handle this situation." And the more they try to handle it, the deeper and deeper they sink. We need to put the marriages in the hands of Jesus. Jesus is a Savior who comes to our rescue. He has what it takes to extricate a marriage from the mud that we've gotten in. He pulled us out and put us back on solid ground, and I praise the Lord for his help. Ever since I let Jesus get involved, I get through the struggles in my marriage. We do not have what it takes to get out unless someone helps to take us out. And that someone is Jesus. He is the mighty God, the everlasting Father, and the Prince of Peace. I'm so glad, friend, Jesus has taken me out of the mud in my marriage. He wants to save you out of the muck and mire of your marriage, clean it up, and put you on holy ground.

A cleaning woman noticed a few bees buzzing around the attic of her home. Since there were only a few, she made no effort to deal with them. Over the summer, the bees continued to fly in and out the attic vent while the woman remained unconcerned, unaware of the growing city of bees that was taking up residence just above her ceiling. The whole attic became a hive, and the ceiling of the second-floor bedroom finally caved in under the weight of hundreds of pounds of honey and thousands of angry bees. While the woman escaped serious injury, she was unable to repair the damage of her accumulated neglect.

Many people's marriages are in this shape because of neglect. We put off dealing with problems. We ignore them until they create a multitude of situations we can't handle. It's too late and our ceiling comes crashing in. Neglect describes the relationship we have with God. Marriage becomes neglected when we pursue other settings. The spouses get neglected. The children get neglected. Responsibilities get neglected. Opportunities get neglected. The family gets neglected. The home gets neglected. When we allow weeds like same-sex marriages, marriage to animals, and marriage to things to grow, the weeds will take over and destroy covenant marriage.

Jesus told a parable about a man who sowed good seed in his field. "But while men slept, his enemy came and sowed tares among the wheat, and went his way. But when the blade was sprung up, and brought forth fruit, then appeared the tares also" (Matt. 13:25).

When a person seeks to be married, knowing that as a single he or she burns with passion, it doesn't have to mean that marriage becomes a channel for the sex drive. A marriage that is going to blessed must exercise self-control. Paul tells us, "But if they cannot contain, let them marry for it is better to marry than to burn" (1 Cor. 7:9). It is better to marry than to burn with passion.

Paul was taking something of the contemporary culture and showing the people how it points to a hunger in the human heart for which the Gospel is the only answer.

God laid the foundation of covenant marriage and marked off its attributes. He stretched a line across it, and if we are ever to enjoy the pleasures of heaven, it must remain in the divine dimensions. Marriage has been sprayed with the hateful gunfire of humanity and riddled with bullets from hell. Humankind has opened the door and yelled out to God, delivering a ton of insults. Undeterred, we march on while singing my boots are made for walking.

According to the Holy Writ, we must consider that something as marvelous and miraculous as covenant marriage needs no accompaniment. We really don't grasp the true nature of marriage that can be blessed, and so often seems to elude us. You see, we think that marriage deals with our happiness and success. A godly marriage is blessed.

1. Blessed is the marriages that has some problems that can be solved in Jesus's name.

2. Blessed are the marriages that last a lifetime.

3. Blessed are the marriages that are strong in spirit, for theirs is the kingdom of heaven.

4. Blessed are those marriage who mourn, for they will be comforted.

5. Blessed are the marriages that meek, for they will inherit the earth.

6. Blessed are the marriages that are merciful, for they shall be shown mercy.

7. Blessed are the marriages who hunger and thirst after righteousness, for they will be filled.

8. Blessed are the marriages that have peacemakers, for they will be called the sons of God.

9. Blessed are the marriages that advocate righteousness, for theirs is the kingdom of heaven.

10. Blessed are marriages that when people insult you, persecute you and falsely say all kinds of evil against you because of me. Rejoice and be glad, because great is your reward in heaven.

11. Blessed are the marriages that are pure in heart, for they will see God.

12. Blessed are the marriages that exercises godly attributes.

God is not in heaven saying let us make a deal, He is in heaven saying that marriage is honorable. Jesus explains this to the Sadducees, who came to Jesus with a question about the resurrection. Moses told us if a man dies without having children, his brother must marry the widow and raise up offspring for him. Now there were seven brothers among us. The first one married and died, and since he had no children, he left his wife to his brother. The same thing happened to the second and third brother, right on down to the seventh. Finally, the woman died. Now then, at the resurrection, whose wife will she be of the seven, since all of them were married to her. "Jesus replied, Ye do err, not knowing the scriptures, nor the power of God. For in the resurrection they neither marry, nor are given in marriage, but are as the angels of God in heaven" (Matt.

22:29–30). "If any of you lack wisdom, let him ask of God, that giveth to all men liberally, and upbraid not; and it shall be given him" (Jas. 1:5).

Serve your marriage wholeheartedly, as if you were serving the Lord, and He will reward you. Whatever I do to my spouse, I do to the Lord. In the ultimate sense, if you want your marriage to be blessed, it has nothing to do with you, but everything to do with your relationship to Jesus Christ. Every time you reach out to your spouse, heaven is watching. Angels will yank the level and give you blessings from the treasure room of heaven. You are storing up for yourselves the treasure of a good foundation for the future so that they may take hold of that which is life indeed (1 Tim. 6:19).

Same-sex couples are often recipients of disdain, verbally attacked and humiliated because of their difference. They no longer must live under a continuous, low-lying black cloud. Jesus can still offer a new life, new desires, hopes, promises, provisions, and purpose. By the mercies of God, they must be persuaded and led to the renewing of the mind, the will of God, which is the good, acceptable, and perfect will of God to be blessed.

Proverbs 22:15 says, "Foolishness is bind in the heart of a child, but the rod of correction will drive it from them." Proverbs 13:24 says, "He that spares his rod hates his son: but he that loveth him chasten him betimes." My parents said, "This is going to hurt me more than it hurts you." God is going to be poured out on wrath.

1. The anger of God is not like our anger.

2. God's wrath is provoked.

3. God is slow to anger.

4. God's wrath is revealed now (Rom. 1:24–28).

5. God's wrath is stored up.

6. God's wrath is on sinners.

God's wrath was poured out on Jesus, and for humanity to avoid the wrath of God, you must accept Jesus as your Savior. God allows wicked sinners to continue enjoying His food, air, health, freedom, and liberty. Humanity has blasphemed His holy name in marriage.

The United States of America was built on the slogan, "In God we trust." But today we no longer abide faithfully by that trust in marriage. The society we live in is bringing the same cruel tyranny and bondage by committing wickedness and tolerating wickedness. Proverbs 14:34 says, "Righteousness exalted a nation: but sin is a reproach to any people." Sin has brought much reproach upon America. The rest of the world views America with disgust, disdain, and distrust. We have become sinful people. What happens in Las Vegas is recorded in Heaven. Marriage looks like two men getting married, two females getting married, or marriage to animals or things. Moral wrong can never be made a godly right. The only marriage that will receive the blessing of the Lord is between a male and a female.

CHAPTER TWELVE

Infidelity In Marriage

Covenant marriage is under the gun, up against the paradoxical times, surrounded by complications, hip-deep in alligators and no way to drain the swamp. You feel yourself getting frustrated when you hear that marriage is in the turbulence of devaluing. When you are searching for significance amid killer bees and you want to keep your faithfulness, work on it.

We are living in a communication revolution: beepers, faxes, the Internet, email, voice mail, answering machines, cellular phones, and all kinds of text messaging. At the same time, we get out of touch with each other.

I submit to you that faithfulness in a covenant marriage is real. It is self-control manifested in a gentle spirit built on an unshakable confidence in God to stay on the right track. What sets us apart from other men/women is a combination of courage, coolness under pressure, and total self-control in a danger zone. We have it, and others do not. So, what do we call faithfulness in a marriage?

We honor the Dirty Harrys of the world, the Rambo's and the Terminators, NBA's best, NFL superstars, the king of pop and rock that do not respect the bond in marriage. We laugh at comedians who flout profanity, cursing, and lying. We watch daily soap operas that are against the rules of life. Many of these shows influence family living with scenes reflecting unfaithful marriage affairs.

Marriage holds times of great joy. "Thy wife shall be as a fruitful vine by the sides of thine house: thy children like olive plants round about thy table" (Ps. 128:3), and it creates the best environment for raising children. Unfaithfulness breaks the bond of trust, the foundation of all relationships. Unfaithfulness has been a trait of humanity. "For God doth know that in the day ye eat thereof, then your eyes shall be opened, and ye shall be as gods, knowing good and evil" (Gen. 3:5). One of the tragic implications of this event is that man lost his status and began to feel a sense of arrogance, inadequacy, and despair, valuing the opinion of others over the truth of God. Teachings apart from God leave immorality, lack of justice, unfaithfulness, and encourage a philosophy that heightens the dignity of humanity. The Scriptures teach that man apart from God is enslaved to sin and condemned to hell. God's response to sin is not condemnation if you are faithful in every area of life, including marriage.

Many married couples enter conflicts, and both come out as losers. Some disputes can leave a feeling of insecurity and anger. There are better ways of coping with infidelity than withdrawing from your spouse. Many married people want to be used mightily by God, and they want to do great things for God. Infidelity in marriage exists and is not going away soon.

God declares that you remain faithful in marriage to be used as a powerful instrument for positive change. He can use you to influence marriage, people at church, people at home, at school, at work, and in your neighborhood. God can use your marriage gifts to change lives. Those who honor the Lord in your marriage, God says, "Wherefore the LORD God of Israel saith, I said indeed that thy house, and the house of thy father, should walk before me forever: but now the LORD saith, be it far from me; for them that honor me I will honor, and they that despise me shall be lightly esteemed" (1 Sam. 2:30).

God has the power to shut the mouths of lions. He has the power to shut down a pagan culture. He has the power to shut down infidelity, but he gives you choices to make decisions that are based on godly principle. Humanity has the imagination of poets, the mind of philosophers, the hand of artists, the tongue of a great singer, but not the hearts of God who created you. Humanity has not learned lessons of faithfulness in covenant marriage.

We continuously are engaged in the things of the flesh, such as immorality, impurity, sensuality, idolatry, sorcery, anger, outbursts, heresies, envying, drunkenness, and running around with the wrong crowd (Gal. 5:19-21). A transformed life in Jesus Christ emulates things which are holy, such as love, joy, peace, patience, kindness, faithfulness gentleness, and self-control (Gal. 5:22–23).

Covenant marriage has become a menace to society because we have let the enemy strike where it hurts the most, the reproduction of men and women made in the image of God, filled with His Spirit. Satan has given teeth to infidelity. God's blessing has always been upon humanity associated with protection, provision, protection, and happiness for the family. His hands guide us in troubled times. "Fear thou not; for I am with thee be not dismayed; for I am thy God: I will strengthen thee; yea, I will help thee; yea, I will uphold thee with the right hand of my righteousness" (Isa. 41:10). "Blessed is the man that walketh not in the counsel of the ungodly, nor stands in the way of sinners, nor sit in the seat of the scornful. But his delight is in the law of the LORD; and in his law doth he meditates day and night. And he shall be like a tree planted by the rivers of water, that bringeth forth his fruit in his season; his leaf also shall not wither; and whatsoever he doeth shall prosper" (Ps. 1:1–3).

When we get married, we are to walk in perfect harmony with God. Genesis 2:17 tells us, "But of the tree of the knowledge of good and evil, thou shalt not eat of it: for in the day that thou eat thereof thou shalt surely die." God's word from the past continues to address a world in the present so that we may return to His plan in marriage. God wanted his truth to get a hold of humans, and humanity must obey His laws.

When you pour out your heart to someone, it becomes difficult when they betray you. A spouse who is involved in infidelity has lost faith in the marriage. Infidelity by a marriage partner is commonly called philandering, adultery, or an affair. What are the causes of infidelity? Many reasons for infidelity are outcomes from education level, personality, opportunity, attachment style, income level and employment, race, culture, religion, and marital satisfaction.

Some research studies suggest that men's and women's rate of infidelity is becoming increasingly similar (Oliver & Hyde, 1993). Men start affairs for sex and women for emotional reasons. Most of these affairs originate from sexual fantasies, secret get-togethers, phone conversations, a passion for time together, which are hidden from the spouse. Infidelity is a result of:

- sex addiction or character flaws in the spouse who chooses to cheat.

- unintentional involvements that develop from friendships.

- problems in the marriage that create an unhappy marriage and the spouse starts looking for something better.

- a spouse engaging in punishing their partner to get even for disliked behavior.

- Being overwhelmed by life circumstances, leading to a way to escape and find comfort.

- a spouse not providing for the needs of the other, like money, transportation, and kindness.

It's estimated that roughly 30 percent to 60 percent of all married individuals (in the United States) would engage in infidelity at some point during their marriage. Commonly quoted statistics suggest that men are unfaithful to their partners than women. And these numbers are probably on the conservative side if you consider that close to half of all marriages end in divorce (people are more likely to stray as relationships fall apart).

Infidelity is present in nearly one-third of all marriages. The concept is not limited to just men, as women, both young and old, are closing in on their male counterparts. Women have become more physically and financially self-supporting than ever, and this can lead to harming a marriage more easily than in the past.

Infidelity is becoming more common among people under 30. Many experts believe this increase in cheating is due to more opportunity (time spent away from a spouse), as well as young people developing the habit of having multiple sexual partners before marriage. The internet, e-mail, and chat rooms are making it easier for people to engage in infidelity. There will be definitive signs of cheating as the marriage progresses. But, in hindsight, you will discover symptoms of infidelity.

Psychologist S. M. Drigotas developed an infidelity scale. The Infidelity Scale is an 11-item scale using 8 points to predict infidelity. It divided reasons of infidelity into five categories: sexuality-emotional satisfaction, social context, attitudes-norms, and revenge-hostility.

According to Mackenzie, sexual infidelity is a relationship with someone outside of the marriage that is purely or primarily sexual (there is little or no emotional attachment). Sexual infidelity in this study wasn't limited to intercourse, and it contains any sexual activity that breaks the trust of sexual exclusivity within a marriage, such as sexual kissing and heavy petting. It includes activities where there is no physical contact at all, such as telephone or online sex, since the offender is investing in sexuality outside of the marriage. It is not accidental, although the actions may have been impulsive due to some degree of ignorance.

A major study at the University of Chicago in 1990 discovered that 25 percent of all marriages are involved in infidelity. Research studies consistently show that 2 percent to 3 percent of children are the product of infidelity. And most of these children are unknowingly raised by men who are not their biological fathers. DNA testing is finally making it easy for people to check the paternity of their children

Joanne Rogers, suggests four ways on *How To forgive A Cheating Husband*:

1. Forgive with intelligence. Be wise because cheaters are likely to cheat again. Do things a little differently this time around until your trust is regained.

2. Figure out the reasons for cheating. Spouses do cheat for reasons to satisfy their ego. Figure out together the reasons for cheating with the help of a therapist. Once you've both figured out the reasons, you'll need to work on them together as a team.

3. Communication is the key to the conversation about how to fix things. The reassurance will instill confidence to help

you forgive. But again, nothing can be done without the first step.

4. The condition of the relationship after several years together will influence the couple's reactions

The first building block of faithfulness in a covenant marriage is honesty. God does not expect you to be perfect, but He expects you to be honest. A spouse acts in the best interests of their partner. Jesus expects you to do for your spouse as he did for his Father. His relationship with His Father is a model for marriage. Jesus always told the truth, being kind and obedient. Faithfulness in your marriage requires that you are honest with your spouse.

The second building block of faithfulness in your marriage is trust. You won't surrender to your spouse unless you believe your spouse. The more you realize how much you love your spouse, the more you realize how much you can trust your partner. Your wife won't follow you unless she trusts you. Make every attempt to regain your spouse's trust.

The third building block is to admit you are wrong and not blame your behavior on your spouse. You have some inadequacies that need special attention. Tackle your problems with sensitivity and smarts. Most couples want to forget and leave the affair in the past. However, the more the unfaithful spouse remembers what happened can have an impact on the future of the marriage. Take the road less traveled when a lot is at stake; it will take moral courage to get back on track.

The fourth step of healing is to deal with the influence of the infidelity. The unfaithful spouse must regret what happens within the framework of infidelity. At the end of treatment, most of the participants had a high level of forgiveness, reacting to the infidelity.

As statistics indicate, more men than women have affairs. Among those men and women who do have affairs, men have more partners than do women. Men who have affairs are more likely to do so without emotional involvement, whereas women's affairs are accompanied by emotional involvement.

Covenant marriage fails because of unfaithfulness of sticking to God's plan of marriage. Satan has laid traps for humanity. I have learned to control the desires for some things that will cause me to become unfaithful in marriage. Faithful men of God always be aware that Satan will lay traps for you. Jesus tells Peter, "But I have prayed for thee, that thy faith fails not: and when thou art converted, strengthen thy brethren" (Lk. 22:32).

God is not in the business of swapping blessings because you are in His favor. Let not your heart grow weary and faint in acting nobly and doing right (Gal. 6:9). I have heard it said, "God won't give you more than you can handle." It's merely a misquotation, "There hath no temptation taken you but such as is common to man: but God is faithful, who will not suffer you to be tempted above that ye are able; but will with the temptation also make a way to escape, that ye may be able to bear it" (1 Cor. 10:13). It appears to be no temptation has overtaken you that is not common to man. God is faithful, and he will not let you be tempted beyond your ability, but with the temptation, he will also provide the way of escape, that you may be able to endure it (1 Cor. 10:13). James states, "Let no man say when he is tempted, I am tempted of God: for God cannot be tempted with evil, neither tempt he any man. But every man is tempted, when he is drawn away of his own lust, and enticed" (Jas 1:13). God does not tempt you but will permit Satan to do so. He gives Satan permission.

Often, we will find ourselves in situations of pleasure and lust that we don't want to handle. Satan is not in the business of sparing anyone. He doesn't care whether you are married or single. If you find yourself in sin, God is not going to dwell therein.

Some couples in the Bible have been involved in infidelity. Norman Vincent Peale, the author of *Bible Stories*, tells us David was a great king of Israel. He had many wives and concubines. All men respected and honored him. David was a man after God's heart, but he fell into dire times. And then this great man made a grievous error. David became involved with another man's wife, and he became unfaithful.

Sometimes we will find ourselves in the wrong place at the right time. David's servant Uriah, the captain of his army, was taking part in the military mission. David should have been on the same mission leading the army, but he remained in Jerusalem. One day David walked out on the roof of his palace and observed a woman bathing in the courtyard of the house nearby. Her beauty overtook him, and he became infatuated. He summoned Bathsheba (Uriah's wife) to the palace and treated her like one of the wives, and she became pregnant. David's unfaithfulness led to other plots to cover the affair. It led to conspiracy, pain, grief, and murder. Each one of us can learn that unfaithfulness in our marriage can be painful. David was involved with Bathsheba. They endured many, many hardships before being powerfully used by God. "But the Lord delivers them out of them all" (Ps. 34:19).

As Christians, if you try to face the battle of infidelity alone, it will be difficult. But when you hand it over to the Lord, He gives you the victory before you even can see it. That's the great God you serve.

Joseph demonstrated a life of faithfulness. Joseph was not married when he was a young man, but he was a man of integrity. He found himself in the wrong place but conducted himself as a man of God at the right time. Joseph was handsome and was notice by Potiphar's wife (Gen. 39:6–7). "And she caught him by his garment, saying, lie with me: and he left his garment in her hand, and fled, and got him out" (Gen. 39:12). Joseph could have lost his faith with Potiphar's wife if he had not been faithful to himself and God. Most men of today, including covenant-married men, would end up in bed with Potiphar's wife. When a person lowers their guard by exposing themselves to acts of infidelity, it will lead to unfaithfulness. First Corinthians 6:18 tells us to flee from sexual immorality. When we are faced with the test of unfaithfulness in our marriage, don't become ensnared. Let's do like Joseph.

Kelly Hamon, author of *The Worship Bulletin Insert, Ways to Strengthen Your Marriage,* offers some resources that will benefit both single and married couples. These twelve tips from the bulletin will encourage simple ideas and concepts to strengthen faithfulness in a covenant marriage.

- Start each day with a kiss. Decide to begin the day with love.

- Always wear your wedding ring and let it be a visual reminder of your commitment.

- Go on a date with your spouse once a week. Even if it's just for coffee, dedicate time for the two of you. Take a walk or watch TV while holding hands.

- Be polite. Are you more polite to coworkers or store clerks than you are to the one you love? Practice good manners at home. End each day giving her hugs. Decide to end the day with love.

- Give gifts. While diamonds are a girl's best friend, a card, a single rose, or a favorite candy bar can also do the trick.

- Laugh together. Find something to laugh about daily and share. Life is complete with laughter.

- Do what your spouse wants before being asked. Anticipate your spouse's needs and jump right in to help. Put his or her needs before your comfort.

- The best way to give support is to encourage your spouse to do his or her best and to feel confident.

- Look your best. Comfort doesn't have to be socks and a T-shirt for bed every night. Watch sunsets together. Find the beauty in life and share it.

- Ask, what can I do to make you happier? You may be surprised at how simple it is to please your spouse.

- Reminisce about your time together. Talk, share, and create new times together.

- Pray for your spouse daily. Don't let a day go by without praying for your marriage, your spouse, and your family. Make it a priority.

One of the great destructions in marriage is infidelity. It is a selfish act of lust. It is a tool of Satan to make fools through the ensuing stupidity, to subvert the honor of marriage. We cannot shape our individuality because we mess up and cannot blame it on anyone. You want to identify a scapegoat to pin it on. You need to look forward to a time when things will become better and less complicated. Find the time and energy to restore your relationship.

It is a tragedy to have something rob your marriage of its sacredness. Commitment and love do endure all disappointment, suffering, and hardship. You have caused your marriage to become dominated by infidelity. Your marriage must touch down in the grace and mercy of the Lord before settling onto the runway. You must stay focused on what is essential. Continue to care for each other. Resolve the issue and don't seek a divorce. Life doesn't promise us that the glass will always be filled. You are responsible for filling it any way you can with all the things necessary for an excellent marriage. The chemistry of life changes as you mature as a couple. Your marriage can improve, and you can be happier. You need to forgive and forget. Look forward too many more anniversaries.

The relationship between spouses is enhanced when both parties can see the value and beauty in the other. Complement each other with gifts and view each other as gifts from God. Furthermore, when God's light shines through both of you, an unstoppable union is formed.

The crux of a successful covenant marriage is in Jesus Christ. Husbands and wives complement one another best when Christ is at the center. There can be no subservient or dictatorial attitudes when Christ is at the center of the marriage. Don't let Satan become a hitchhiker in your marriage. It's time to tell him to get out.

CHAPTER THIRTEEN

Transforming Covenant Marriage In A Contemporary Society

A difficult task for most generations is to establish a theological foundation of marriage extracted from Bible beliefs, with emphasis on the word of God for today's society. Scripture states, The Lord directed the teaching of the commandments and decrees, and to observe in the land that you will possess. So, that your children, after them may fear the Lord your God. if you live by keeping the decrees and commandments that I give, you may enjoy longevity (Deut. 6:2).

Biblical transformation means to change or renewal from a life that no longer conforms to the ways of the world to ones that pleases God (Rom. 12:2). You will accomplish this by the renewing of your minds to an inward spiritual transformation that will manifest itself in outward actions. A transformed life in Christ is demonstrated by bearing fruit in every good work and growing in the knowledge of God (Col. 1:10). Transformation involves those who were once far from God and are now being drawn near to Him through the blood of Christ (Eph. 2:13). A transition is defined as a passage from one ending state to another beginning state.

Covenant marriage is being attacked and represents one of the most difficult challenges that churches in this generation will face. People are struggling with same-sex attractions, and men and women are struggling with gender confusion. A biblical response to these challenges will be required. New skills of compassion and understanding, inside and outside the congregation, must be established. Same-sex marriage has birthed out of Western society and becomes a challenge to the institution of marriage and redefines sexuality and normalize sex relationships. The sexual revolution is not going away. The Church must continue to move forward with biblical fidelity that is clear, and Christian compassion to transform broken lives. Matthew 9:36 says, "But when he saw the multitudes, he was moved with compassion on them, because they fainted, and were scattered abroad, as sheep having no shepherd."

God knows what all generations need. Presently, this generation is disobeying godly principles and robbing themselves of His blessings in covenant marriage. How can a generation know God without hearing and learning more about God? The transformation of marriage seeks to assess and affirm that same-sex marriage, marriage to animals and things, is not correct. Marriage is sacred and will always be if humanity exists. The younger generations are accepting same-sex marriage because they are not as heavily involved with religion. Religion gets in the way of equal rights.

All generations need to be taught from previous generations the importance of obtaining a covenant marriage relationship. Many times, humanity needs to change some habits and realize if things are going to become better, some changes are required. It must be understood that for each generation to survive, we must work together to pass on those truths that work. We live in a world together as one body.

Now the body is not made up of one part, but of many. If the foot should say, because I am not a hand, I do not belong to the body. It would not, for that reason, cease to be part of the body. And if the ear should say, because I am not an eye, I do not belong to the body. It will not, for that reason, cease to be part of the body. If the entire body were an eye, where would the sense of hearing be? If the body was an ear, where would the sense of hearing be? If the whole body were a nose, where would the sense of smell be? God has arranged the parts of the body, every one of them, just as he wanted them to be. If they were all one part, where would the body be? As it is, there are many parts, but one body. The eye cannot say to the hand; I don't need you. And the hand cannot reply to the feet; I don't need you. On the contrary, those parts of the body that seems to be weaker are indispensable, and the parts that we think are less honorable we treat with special honor (1 Cor. 12:12–23).

It's becoming alarming that children view programs on TV that display same-sex marriage relationships. They are getting used to it. I believe gay celebrities play a huge role in the process. Ellen and Neil Patrick Harris are examples of icons today that influence generations of teens who loves them! It's also a fact that people are becoming less attached to religion, but even religion is changing. It's starting to become more welcoming to new ideas, such as same-sex marriage, because of the laws passed recently.

We are living at times people are becoming open-minded and seem to accept the idea of same-sex marriage and less acceptable is a covenant marriage. People are becoming informed and understanding that other people have the right to marry whomever they choose. The media is becoming more involved in releasing advertisements involving same-sex couples taking the lead. Same-sex marriage cannot save the institution of marriage; it will damage it. It is not right to allow people of the same sex to get married, because this is fundamentally contradictory to the idea of covenant marriage. Allowing people to call non-traditional pairings marriage is disrespectful to God.

The Scriptures continue to speak to generations as they reject God's plan for covenant marriage. The understanding of marriage does not mean total conformity and uniformity to contemporary idealism. When humanity comes to its senses and returns to the common denominator, it will make sense again in this world that we need to transform covenant marriage in a contemporary society back to God's plan.

Theologian JA Van der Ven tells us, "One of the traditional approaches that the Church has adopted regards to moral formation is the transmission and impartation of the normative values found in the Bible. If young people are given the right knowledge, they will perform the right action, according to their understanding. If these realities are practiced and keep in mind, they will likely continue to make the right moral decisions.

Therefore, each generation has a responsibility to receive the preaching and teachings of God. Each generation must be present to learn. "And be not conformed to this world: but be ye transformed by the renewing of your mind, that ye may prove what is that good, and acceptable, and perfect, will of God" (Rom. 12:2).

Among those attending church, covenant marriage is essential to Christians. The same proportion of non-Christians say, "It is not relevant to me personally." The non-Christians' reasoning is an indicator that some teaching will be essential to help facilitate a transformative connection with God's plan for covenant marriage.

The minds of young adults need a transformation of moral ethics if marriage is going to be transformed. It is a challenge for contemporary society. While most teens have a reputation as gamers, use of laptops, TVs, and of course, smartphones, still reigns supreme. Seventy-eight percent of teens use a smartphone. Sixty-nine percent of teens use a computer. Sixty-eight percent watch television. Sixty-two percent use a gaming console. Fifty-two percent use a tablet.

Many teens and young adults are rushing headlong into a sexual revolution, and it is creating problems resulting from being exposed to the expression of the media and making same-sex marriages a norm. Marriage has always been a covenant between a man and a woman for the well-being of procreation. Same-sex marriages oppose the social order for the following reasons:

1. Is it really a marriage between two men and two women?
2. It violates natural laws (Rom. 1:26–27).
3. It denies a child of a father and mother.
4. It promotes and validates homosexuality.
5. It turns a moral wrong into a civil right.
6. It does not create a family but a union that will not produce children.
7. It defeats the purpose of covenant marriage (God's plan for marriage).
8. It imposes an acceptable behavior on society.
9. It's a sexual revolution with deadly forthcoming.
10. It offends a Holy God.

Generation Z was born between 1999 and 2015, making the oldest of them 18 this year. Most of them are in their teens and childhood years. Gen Z is the second-largest generation alive today. In the US, there are 69 million of them, compared to 66 million millennials, 55 million Gen Xers and 76 million boomers. The parents of Gen Z are Gen X, and millennials are the most ethnically diverse generation alive today. They have, for better or worse, grown up with technology at their fingertips. The smartphone was invented before most of them were even born.

George Barna, the author of the book *Generations Next,* defines a set of rules focusing on the mindset of Generation X, which includes those born between 1965 and 1978.

1. Personal relationships count and institutions don't.
2. Enjoy people, and life opportunities are more important than productivity.
3. They believe change is good.
4. Don't waste searching for absolutes. There are none.
5. Spiritual truth may take many forms.
6. Express your rage.

The Barna study finds that many of them have not even been exposed to Christianity or church. There are a lot of churches that are empty in this country. Gen Z is the one that is missing in action. There are many of them that are spiritually blind. For the first time in our nation's history, that is becoming more common.

In America, we enjoy our constitutional freedoms while we reject Christian ethics. I don't know a lot about Russia, but I do know they do not treat everyone equally. The social justice craze is building a hyper-restrictive culture of political correctness. The thoughts and actions of people have changed with the change of time. The institution of covenant marriage can only be transformed by teaching people to make better decisions in their adult life. It comes down to transforming young minds.

The family structure has changed. Nothing is done to encourage unity in the family. God wants the transformation of covenant marriage to connect in love, respect, romance, and spiritual oneness between a man and a woman. We need to restore commitment in a covenant marriage because it is exclusive. The equalizer is Jesus when we come together to get married. He is with us. In Matthew's Gospel, Jesus makes an incredible promise to us, "For where two or three are gathered together in my name, there am I in the midst of them" (Matt. 18:20). But He is not in a same-sex marriage relationship, marriage to animals and to things.

Market research firm *The Gild* discovered that the mindset of Generation Z is more conservative than millennials on gay issues. The Church should rejoice at the survey. The group concludes people born since 2001 are shaping up to be more conservative than anybody since the post-war generation. Fifty-nine percent of young people responding to the survey said their opinions on same-sex marriage, transgender rights, and marijuana were either "conservative" or "moderate" – a drastic swing from millennials and members of Generation X. The survey revealed that 80 percent were either "quite liberal" or "very liberal." Generation Z was also more likely to say they "hate" tattoos and unusual body piercings (11 percent) and prefer to save money rather than spend it (47 percent).

Teenagers today are the most non-Christian generation in American history, as only 4 out of 100 teens holds a correct biblical worldview and 1 out of every 8 teens identifies as non-heterosexual, a new survey released by one of the nation's leading evangelical polling firms has found. The Pew Research Center reported among the older cohorts, boomers (ages 51 to 69) are currently divided (45 percent favor, 48 percent oppose). The silent group (ages 70 to 87) are the only generation in which 53 percent oppose and 39 percent favor gay marriage. But for both groups, same-sex marriage has increased over the past decade (9 percentage points among boomers, 16 percentage points among the silent).

Are you guilty of believing in same-sex marriage? Is God in complete control of your marriage? "Finally, brethren, whatsoever things are true, whatsoever things are honest, whatsoever things are just, whatsoever things are pure, whatsoever things are lovely, whatsoever things are of good report; if there be any virtue, and if there be any praise, think on these things. Those things, which ye have both learned, and received, and heard, and seen in me, do and the God of peace shall be with you" (Phil. 4:8–9).

The transformation of covenant marriage will be renewed back to its place in society when godly instructions are grounded in the teachings of God's word. We are entreated to present covenant marriage as a living sacrifice to God. "And we know that all things work together for good to them that love God, to them who are the called according to his purpose" (Rom. 8:28). Same-sex marriage or marriage to animals and things contrasts with holy living. There must be removal of such unlikeness. To offer your bodies as a living sacrifice, holy and pleasing to God, there must be a true and proper mind transformation.

Transformation does not happen overnight. Regeneration is instantaneous, but our transformation is continuous as we conform to covenant marriage in the image of God's plan. A renewed mind begins with changing the behavior with a measure of faith in God. We come to the conclusions:

1. God is the ultimate authority in a covenant marriage.

2. You are held accountable in a covenant marriage.

3. God uses marriage to carry out his useful purpose on earth.

4. You are to be obedient to the vows of marriage.

5. God does not define you according to culturally defined externals. Gender, ethnicity, and family heritage is essential to God.

The word of God must be taught. It is illegal to possess a Bible in some foreign countries. So, some believers had a small collection of Scriptures. They tore them up in little pieces and distributed them among the body of believers. The plan was to memorize the portion they had been given, then the next time they met, they would redistribute the pieces.

They believed that marriage was between a man and a woman and instituted by God with Adam and Eve. Genesis 2:24 states: "Therefore shall a man leave his father and his mother and shall cleave unto his wife: and they shall be one flesh." Each time these believers arrived inconspicuously in small groups throughout the day, to not arouse the suspicion of informers. They closed the windows and locked doors. They began by singing hymns quietly with deep emotion. Suddenly, the door was pushed open, and two soldiers walked in with loaded automatic weapons ready to shoot. One shouted, "Everybody line up against the wall and was asked to renounce their commitment to marriage of a man and a female, may leave now!" Two, three quickly left, then another. After a few more seconds, two more left.

The announcement came, "This is your last chance. Either turn against your faith in marriage established by God or stay and suffer the consequences." Finally, two more in embarrassed silence covered their faces and slipped out into the night. Only a few were left. Parents with small children trembling beside them looked down reassuringly. They fully expected to be gunned down or, at best, to be imprisoned.

After a few moments of complete silence, the soldier closed the door, looked back at those who stood against the wall and said, "Keep your hands up but this time in praise to our Lord Jesus Christ. I have learned by experience, however, that unless people are willing to die for their faith, they cannot fully be trusted.

The question is, "Ah Lord GOD! behold, thou hast made the heaven and the earth by thy great power and stretched out arm, and there is nothing too hard for thee?" (Jer. 37:17). The answer to this critical question is there is nothing too hard for God (Jer. 32:17). We're tried everything except God's way to transform a society back to covenant marriage.

We try advertising, publicizing, organizing, fighting, voting, and got permission from humanity to defraud God. Today, the abnormal is considered the norm. Society has tons of trash to unload. We are making attempts to make covenant marriage seem weird and trashy. As popular as it may appear, the gates of hell will never prevail against covenant marriage.

CHAPTER FOURTEEN

The Reasonability of Covenant Marriage

The reasonability of marriage must return within its boundaries. Sometimes when we hear the word *boundaries*, we look at it as a bad thing. But anything that does not have boundaries is not clearly defined and sooner or later will ultimately stretch beyond its limitations.

How do we overcome the views that have become sensitive, complex, and philosophical? Marriage has gone through some appalling, scandalous changes and has lost its luster for spiritual inspiration and is now dripping with the constitutional embracement of human rights. It was once a clean institution, but now it looks like dirty laundry.

The three significant events in family life are birth, marriage, and death. Marriage was regarded as the most important. The loss of marriage morality has created a problem in this nation and marriage has lost it mission. Marriage has become a protective institutional bubble regressing from a godly model to human-made employment. The encroachment of postmodernism has caused many Christians to morph into protective harbors or holy huddles in a safe environment. They can dwell together without fear of the world's secularization knocking at the doors to gain permanent entry.

The marriage experience of today is different than that of Mom and Dad's. When minds are destroyed in this present generation, society is in trouble. The modern age does not fear God's plan for marriage. They do not look to give logical, analytical reasons but continue to enjoy the freedom of choice. Many feel the Church is not offering answers to these problems.

We must recognize that revolutionary change has come to marriage. Once a harmonious relationship existed between the government, education, and the Church. They were united in their adherence to the Christian faith.

Marriage is unchurched in a post-Christian culture. Well-established values are unpacking, from coast to coast, and impacting the churched communities and beyond. The "unchurched" is the broader category of those who do not attend a church on a regular or continual basis.

Societal norms once viewed as established are dismissed as inappropriate in a post-Christian era. Why is covenant marriage becoming a lost institution? We need to investigate some issues in marriage through life standards and devotional practices and offer a delicious assortment of valuable knowledge that is practical and critical in this era.

Same-sex marriage is wrong in the eyes of God, which can be argued by some people to be righteous. But there are tons of Scriptures in the Bible to which we don't pay attention. I oppose the idea of same-sex marriage, and with animals and things. I have strong religious beliefs which have shaped my life, and it gives me reasons to oppose this matter. I can honestly say the only relationship that is productive is between a male and a female. The emotion generated by sexual contact that warrants a critical decision between a man and woman is not a complicated one, but in any other fashion will create significant consequences. God laid down a plan of marriage between male and female as a foundational law.

The atheist is pushing immoral content to the entire world through social media, laws, and the internet. I believe this is a slap in God's face. Many people have become a satanic tool to corrupt Christian people! How sad is that! God is going to bring wrath on this world. Same-sex marriage is another way Satan is destroying humanity. Paul tells us, "O foolish Galatians, who hath bewitched you, that ye should not obey the truth, before whose eyes Jesus Christ hath been evidently set forth, crucified among you? Are ye so foolish? Having begun in the Spirit, are ye now made perfect by the flesh" (Gal. 3:1, 3). "Stand fast therefore in the liberty wherewith Christ hath made us free and be not entangled again with the yoke of bondage" (Gal. 5:1).

More Christians need to voice some sentiments about the traditional approach and contemporary approach to marriage. Marriage can be successful one couple at a time. We live in a world where knowing the past and present makes it our best choice to construct the future. God's plan provides proof that His way is always excellent for marriage.

Humanity has extended personal boundaries which should never be established. Covenant marriage should never be violated. Marriage should be betrothed with integrity and respect for God.

Satan is the author of extramarital affairs, same-sex marriages, marriage to animals and things. These boundaries will destroy covenant marriage. They must be torn down, making it more honorable. Let wisdom, patience, understanding, forgiveness, love, and peace abide in every marriage to weather the storms and stay committed to the covenant of marriage.

"Finally, my brethren, be strong in the Lord, and in the power of his might. Put on the whole armor of God, that ye may be able to stand against the wiles of the devil. For we wrestle not against flesh and blood, but against principalities, against powers, against the rulers of the darkness of this world, against spiritual wickedness in high places. Wherefore take unto you the whole armor of God, that ye may be able to withstand in the evil day, and having done all, to stand. Stand therefore, having your loins girt about with truth, and having on the breastplate of righteousness, and your feet shod with the preparation of the gospel of peace. Above all, taking the shield of faith, wherewith ye shall be able to quench all the fiery darts of the wicked. And take the helmet of salvation, and the sword of the Spirit, which is the word of God. Praying always with all prayer and supplication in the Spirit and watching thereunto with all perseverance and supplication for all saints" (Eph. 6:10–18).

God's people are being led by the personal interests of the world and not helping to overcome this evil inclination of same-sex marriage and marriage to animals and things. The government is shaping the way we live. You end up fighting over doctrine instead of fighting the real enemy, Satan and his demonic rebels.

The body of Christ lacks unity and faith against such mayhem. Some practices influence salvation and eternal destination. The Church has become divided and is hiding its light under bushel basket. The Church is sitting back while Satan is allowing liberal politicians, media, advocates, and evolutionists to take control and undermine sound biblical doctrine. They poison the minds of the younger generations and society. Jesus is coming back for his bride, who is without spot and wrinkle, and Christians must be one of those brides (Eph. 5:27).

Some critics believe that covenant marriage law is the government's way of giving its official permission to a religious form of marriage. Those who oppose the idea of covenant marriage have described the practice as an example of religion harnessing state power, and to mean a contract that is entered between man and God. The couple agrees to live together as husband and wife for as long as they both live.

NOTES

INTRODUCTION

1. Mike McDaniel, Case Studies of Selected Missional Churches That Examine Strategies Used to Engage the Unchurched in Post-Christendom Context. D. Min. diss., Dallas Theological Seminary, 2010, 17-18.

CHAPTER 1. A Descriptive View of Marriage

1. Growing in Grace, Daily Devotional, http://www. parkgatebaptistchurch.com/daily_devotional.html (accessed on February 4, 2017).

2. Definition of marriage, https://www.merriam-webster.com/ dictionary/marriage (accessed on April 30, 2019).

3. The Impending Supreme Court Decision on Marriage – A Resource for Preaching, http://www.usccb.org/prayer-and-worship/homiletics/upload/Homily-Helps-for-SCOTUS-2015.pdf (accessed on June 15, 2018).

4. Timothy and Kathy Keller, *The Meaning of Marriage: Facing the Complexities of Commitment with the Wisdom of God* (New York: Dutton Publishing, 2008), 17.

5. Peter Clarke, Social Media and Attacks on Traditional, Investigative Journalism, FindLaw. https://blogs.findlaw.com/technologist/2017/02/social-media-and-attacks-on-traditional-investigative-journalism.html (accessed on June 21, 2017).

6. James E. Faust, The Enriching of Marriage, The Church of Latter-Day Saints, https://www.lds.org/general-conference/1977/10/the-enriching-of-marriage?lang=eng (accessed on July 12, 2018).

7. Blaine Fowers, *Beyond the Myth of Marital Happiness* (San Francisco, CA: Jossey-Bass, 2000), 72.

CHAPTER 2 THE Marriage Covenant

1. James E. Faust, The Enriching of Marriage, https://www.lds.org/general-conference/1977/10/the-enriching-of-marriage?lang=eng (Accessed February 20, 2019).

2. Girlfriend wants to get married, but I don't, https://www.reddit.com/r/Marriage/comments/81unhu/girlfriend_wants_to_get_married_but_i_dont/ (accessed on May 1, 2019).

3. J. W. Hayford, *The Spirit-Filled Family: Holy Wisdom to Build Happy Homes* (Nashville: Thomas Nelson).

4. Ashley and Michael's Covenant, FamilyLife, https://cdn2-www.familylife.com/articles/topics/marriage/getting-married/engagements-and-weddings/ashley-and-michaels-covenant/ (accessed on June 1, 2018).

5. THE COVENANT OF MARRIAGE, Owonike Blog. https://owonike.blogspot.com/2013/02/the-covenant-of-marriage.html (accessed on June 18, 2017).

6. Marriage as a Blood Covenant? The Aquila Report, https://www.theaquilareport.com/marriage-as-a-blood-covenant/ (accessed on January 23, 2018).

7. Webster's Dictionaries, s.v. "cathexis," accessed October 22, 2013, //www.websterdictionaries.com/definition/english/cathexis (accessed on February 24, 2018).

8. Gregory Michael Howe, *The Book of Common Prayer, The Episcopal Church* (New York, NY: Church Publishing Incorporated, 2007), 423–424.

9. Jason Vinson, "7 Signs of Commitment"7, sermons.org. http://www.sermons.org/sermons/vinson1.html (accessed on March 3, 2018).

10. Ancient Marriage, Bible History Online, https://www.Bible-history.com/biblestudy/marriage.html (accessed on November 1, 2018).

11. Authority of Believers, God Gives Authority to Man, http://www.willghormley-maker.com/AuthorityOfBelievers.html (accessed on December 1, 2018).

CHAPTER 3. AN ETERNAL UNION (MALE AND FEMALE)

1. Michael Warner, *The Trouble with Normal: Sex, Politics, and the Ethics of Queer Life* (New York: The Free Press, 1999), 81–147.

2. MARRIAGE IN CONTEMPORARY SOCIETY, Newman Center at Cal-techhttp://www.cco.caltech.edu/~nmcenter/

love/Love_for_Life/LfL.17.html (accessed on January 15, 2018).

3. Margot Carmichael Lester, When Things Go Wrong, Stay above your Faults, Monster Worldwide. https://www.monster.com/career-advice/article/win-the-blame-game (accessed August 23, 2018).

4. Same-Sex Marriage: Does It Meet with God's Approval, Beyond Today, https://www.ucg.org/the-good-news/same-sex-marriage-does-it-meet-with-gods-approval (accessed on February 25, 2018).

5. Giovanna Boldrini, 9 Absolutely Horrifying Marriage Tips from the 1950s, https://www.littlethings.com/marriage-tips-from-the-1950s (accessed on July 18, 2018).

6. Melvin Rhodes, Same-Sex Marriage: Does It Meet with God's Approval? Beyond Today. https://www.ucg.org/the-good-news/same-sex-marriage-does-it-meet-with-gods-approval (accessed on June 25, 2019).

7. Douglas Farrow, Thirteen Theses on Marriage, October 2012, First Things https://www.firstthings.com/article/2012/10/thirteen-theses-on-marriage (accessed on January 15, 2018).

8. Paul R Stevens, *Married for Good* (Downers Grove, Ill. Regent College Publishing, 1986), 17.

9. Andreas Köstenberger, facing marriage problems today, biblical foundation, http://www.biblical founda-tions.org/the top-ten-issues-facing-marriage-and-family-in-today-an-assessment/ (assessed on April 21, 2018).

CHAPTER 4. MAKING CHOICES

1. Shaunti Feldhahn & Robert Lewis, The Wonderful Differences Between Men and Women, crosswalk.com. https://www.crosswalk.com/family/marriage/the-wonderful-biblical-differences-between-men-and-women.html (accessed on April 17, 2017).

2. Donald E. Gowan, *From Eden to Babel: A Commentary on the Book of Genesis 1–11* (Grand Rapids, MI: W. B. Eermands Publisher, 1998), 48.

3. G. J. Wenham, *Genesis 1-15, Vol 1* (Dallas, TX: Word Inc., 1998), 70.

4. When A Wife Is Hardest to Love, She Needs It Most, Marriage Mission International. https://marriagemissions.com/when-a-wife-is-hardest-to-love-she-needs-it-most/ (accessed on May 21, 2019).

5. The Qualities of a Godly Mate, Bible.org. https://Bible.org/seriespage/12-qualities-godly-mate (accessed on April 18, 2019).

6. AYODELE ADEOYE, THE SWORDLESS DEBORAH, https://christiancouplesforum.com/forums/topic/the-swordless-deborah/ (accessed on February 18, 2019).

7. Johny Nathad, Woman - Become More and Truly Beautiful to God, https://www.slideshare.net/jsndaan?utm_campaign=profiletracking&utm_medium=sssite&utm_source=ssslideview (accessed on May 1, 2019).

8. Wisdom and Wealth (Part II), Bible.org. https://Bible.org/series/epistle-st-paul-romans/Lumina.Bible.org?page=58 (accessed on June 25, 2018).

9. Douglas Farrow, Thirteen Theses on Marriage, First Things, https://www.firstthings.com/article/2012/10/thirteen-theses-on-marriage (accessed on March 25, 2018).

10. Nancy Morgan, What Makes a Woman Beautiful? Beyond To-day. https://www.ucg.org/beyond-today/what-makes-a-woman-beautiful (accessed on June 12, 2017).

11. Characteristics of A godly Marriage (1 Peter 3:1–7), Bible.org. https://Bible.org/seriespage/11-characteristics-godly-marriage-1-peter-31-7 (accessed on March 12, 2019).

12. Nancy Morgan, What Makes a Woman Beautiful? https://www.ucg.org/beyond-today/what-makes-a-woman-beautiful (accessed July 22, 2017).

13. THE 25 BEST-PAYING JOBS FOR WOMEN RIGHT NOW, *Forbes Magazine*, https://www.forbes.com/pictures/fgdd45fiji/the-25-best-paying-jobs/#57b9ad686209 (accessed on April 20, 2019).

14. Model for Marriage, Bible.org., https://Bible.org/seriespage/13-model-marriage (accessed on October 18, 2018).

15. W. Spalding, I.H. Evans, Oliver Montgomery, J. Lamar McElhany, The Ministry, https://www.ministrymagazine.org/archive/1933/09/performing-the-marriage-ceremony (accessed on September 2018).

16. Paul Canning, PhD, *Big Idea Sermons* (Nashville, TN: B & H Publishing, 2018), 219.

17. Ngina Otiende, 5 Ways to Love Your Husband Through Every Marriage Season, International Today, https://intentionaltoday.com/5-ways-to-love-your-husband-through-every-season-3/ (accessed on June 5, 2018).

18. Michael Kercheval, Six Ways to Love Your Wife, https://www.fufillingyourvows.com/6-ways-to-love-your-wife/ (accessed on June 5, 2018).

CHAPTER 5. WHERE IS YOUR SERVANT ATTITUDE?

1. A.M. Ariyo, 2005. Some Determinants and Consequences of Marital Instability in Ogun State: A case study, *Nigerian Journal of Applied Psychology*, 8/9, 2/1, 54–69.

2. D. W. Mace, *Close companions: The marriage enrichment handbook* (New York, NY: Continuum, 1982).

3. Webster's, "selfishness," https://www.merriam-webster.com/dictionary/selfish (accessed on May 16, 2019).

4. REMEMBER YOUR CREATOR IN THE DAYS OF YOUR YOUTH!" www.nnedaog.org/SERMONS/SERMEM7.HTM (accessed on November 5, 2018).

5. What Is the Effect of Anger in Relationships? wiseGEEK, https://www.wisegeek.com/what-is-the-effect-of-anger-in-relationships.htm (accessed on April 22, 2019).

6. What Is the Effect of Anger in Relationships? wiseGEEK. https://www.wisegeek.com/what-is-the-effect-of-anger-in-relationships.htm (accessed on September 20, 2018).

7. Patricia Love, ed. d, and Steven Stosny, Ph.D., *How to improve your marriage without talking about it* (New York: Broadway Books, 2007), 2.

8. Violet Woodhouse and Lina Gullen, *Divorce & Money* (Berkley, CA: Bang Publishing, 2017), 21.

9. Inviting God to Your Wedding, beliefnet, https://www.beliefnet.com/entertainment/2000/06/inviting-god-to-your-wedding.aspx (accessed on January 22, 2019).

10. . Melvin Rhodes, Same-Sex Marriage: Does It Meet with God's Approval? UCG.org / Good News, https://www.ucg.org/the-good-news/same-sex-marriage-does-it-meet-with-gods-approval (accessed February 5, 2017).

11. Murray Campbell, Same-Sex Marriage: What Does the Bible Really Have to Say? https://au.thegospelcoalition.org/article/same-sex-marriage-what-does-the-Bible-really-have-to-say/ (accessed on November 25, 2018).

12. Survey: Certified Divorce Financial Analyst® (CDFA®) professionals Reveal the Leading Causes of Divorce, https://institutedfa.com/Leading-Causes-Divorce/ v. 61, No. 4, Oct. 2012 (accessed June 1, 2019).

13. John Gottman, Do All Couples Fight? *Psychology Today.* https://www.psychologytoday.com/us/blog/resolution-not-conflict/201307/marriage-arguments-can-all-conflicts-be-resolved (accessed March 4, 2019).

14. Divorce and Effects on Children, Children- and-Divorce. com., https://www.children-and-divorce.com/divorce-and-effects-on-children.html (accessed on June 30, 2019).

15. Deshpande, Anuradha, and Neelam Pandey. "Psychological Impact of Parental Divorce on Children: A Qualitative Study." *Indian Journal of Health and Wellbeing*, vol. 5, no. 10, Indian Association of Health, Research and Welfare, Oct. 2014, p. 1201.

16. Matthew Jacobson, Faithful Man, https://faithfulman.com/about/ (accessed July 18, 2019).

17. Christina D Richardson and Lee A. Rosen, (1999). School-based interventions for children of divorce. *Professional School Counseling*, 3, (1), 21-27. https://files.eric.ed.gov/fulltext/ED456346.pdf (accessed June 12, 2018).

18. L. Steinberg and SM Dornbusch, 1991, pp. 365–367 (Bee & Boyd, 2004).

CHAPTER 6. THE PROBLEM REMEMBER

1. Jerome Nathanson, *The Ethics of Marriage: Understanding Ethical Religion*. Ed. Howard (Radest, New York, NY. American Ethical Union 17), 145–15.

2. Fred Lowery, *Covenant Marriage* (West Monroe, LA: Howard Publishing Company, 2002), 199.

3. R. A. Animasahun & O. O. Oladeni, Effects of Assertiveness Training and Marital Communication Skills in Enhancing Marital Satisfaction among Baptist Couples in Lagos State, Nigeria, vol. 12, no.14, *Global Journals Inc.* (USA), 2012, https://pdfs.sematicscholar.org/33a1/d7b95514925b64dc733d9139c16c6f7cfc18.pdf.vol. 5, no. 10, Indian Association of Health, Research and Welfare, Oct. 2014, p. 1201.

4. Richard Dowis, *The Lost Art of the Great Speech* (New York: AMA Publications, 2000), 210–11.

5. B. L. Fisher, P. R. Giblin, and M. H. Hoopes, 1982. Healthy family functioning. *Journal of Marriage and Family Therapy*. 8, 273–284.

6. Marriage: Duel or Duet? Sermon by Adrian Rogers, James 3:5 .... https://www.sermoncentral.com/sermons/marriage-duel-or-duet-adrian-rogers-sermon-on-marriage-commitment-165686 (accessed on June 7, 2018).

7. Fred Lowery, *Covenant Marriage* (West Monroe, LA: Howard Publishing Company, 2002), 183.

8. Patricia Love, ed. d, and Steven Stosny, PhD, *How to improve your marriage without talking about it* (New York: Broadway Books, 2007), 2.

9. Howard J. Markman, Scott M. Stanley and Susan L. Blumberg, *Fighting for Your Marriage*, 3rd ed. (San Francisco, CA: Jossey-Bass, 2010), 102.

10. E. A. Akinade 1997. *Towards satisfactory marriage: A marital guidance counselor's approach.* Ibadan: Caltop (publications) Nig. Ltd. (accessed on October 2018).

CHAPTER 7. THE PROBLEM REMEMBER

1. Lesson 4 – Young Adults | Kingdom of Christ. http://www.kingdomofchrist.info/somp5l4/ (accessed on March 3, 2018).

2. Wayne Davis, Lesson 4 – Young Adults, Kingdom of Christ, http://www.kingdomofchrist.info/somp5l4/ (accessed on May 5, 2019).

3. Robert McLaughlin, Prosperity Special, part 4: The divine design in the differences between men and women. https://gbible.org/daily-message/prosperity-special-part-4-divine-design-differences-men-women-phi-49-psa-113-1co-117-12-1pe-31-7-sol-3-1-4-41-5-eph-533/ (accessed on July 23, 2018).

4. Jerome Nathanson, *The Ethics of Marriage: Understanding Ethical Religion.* Ed. Howard (Radest, New York, NY. American Ethical Union 17), 145–15.

5. REMEMBER YOUR CREATOR IN THE DAYS OF YOUR YOUTH, http://www.nnedaog.org/SERMONS/SERMEM7.HTM (accessed May 2, 2019).

6. MONEY MATTERS INTRODUCTION - mtlibertycpchurch. org. http://www.mtlibertycpchurch.org/pdf/sermons/James/ Jam08-14.pdf (accessed on February 7, 2019).

7. Marriage Duel or Duet? - Love Worth Finding with Adrian Rogers, http://www.oneplace.com/ministries/love-worth-finding/read/articles/marriage-due (accessed on April 6, 2017).

8. Barbara Calloway, Dear Female Preachers (Carol Stream, Ill: Tyndale Publishers, Inc., 2011), 121-123.

9. Bad (humorous) marriage advice, ableToknow https:// able2know.org/topic/79229-1 (accessed June 12, 2017).

10. Timothy Williams and Elizabeth Dias, United Methodists Tighten Ban on Same-Sex Marriage and Gay Clergy, https:// www.nytimes.com/2019/02/26/us/united-methodists-vote. html (accessed on March 26, 2019).

CHAPTER 8. WHERE DO YOU STAND?

1. Paul Canning, PhD, *Big Idea Sermons* (Nashville, TN: B & H Publishing, 2018), 221.

2. How Did Mankind Fall from Grace to Sin? - Bible Sprout. https://www.biblesprout.com/articles/Bible/creation/fall-man/ (accessed on October 1, 2018).

3. The Battle for Self-Control - intouch.org. https://www. intouch.org/Watch/Sermon-Series/expressing-godly-character/the-battle-for-self-control (accessed February 17, 2018).

4. Marriage Duel or Duet? - Love Worth Finding with Adrian Rogers, http://www.oneplace.com/ministries/

love-worth-finding/read/articles/marriage-due (accessed on April 6, 2017).

5. Chuck Swindoll, Insights on Marriage and Divorce, one-place. https://www.oneplace.com/ministries/insights-on-marriage-and-divorce/read/articles/what-the-Bible-says-about-lust-15048.html (accessed on May 17, 2019).

6. Mike Mobley. Is Marriage Only Between A Man and A Woman? https://www.beforethecross.com/biblical-teachings/marriage-is-between-a-man-and-a-woman/ (accessed on May 1, 2019).

7. President Obama Supports Same-Sex Marriage | whitehouse. gov. https://obamawhitehouse.archives.gov/blog/2012/05/09/president-obama-supports-same-sex-marriage (accessed on May 12, 2018).

8. Same-Sex Marriage, State by State | Pew Research Center. https://www.pewforum.org/2015/06/26/same-sex-marriage-state-by-state/ (accessed on June 1, 2018).

9. 20 years ago, Bill Clinton signed Defense of Marriage Act, The Washington Times, https://www.washingtontimes.com/news/2016/sep/21/20-years-ago-bill-clinton-signed-defense-of-marria/ (accessed on August 12, 2018).

10. Same-sex marriage - uwgb.eduwww.uwgb.edu/clampitp/Phils Site/Internet (accessed on July 2, 2017).

11. J. E. Yang, (1996, July 13). House votes to curb gay marriages; Bitter debate precedes lopsided outcome; Clinton would sign the bill. The Washington Post, A01.

12. Bidstrup, 2009, Gay Marriage, The Arguments and the Motives, http//www.bidstrup.com/marriage.htm (accessed on March 1, 2019).

13. Brian Tashman, Pat Robertson: Gay Marriage Will Lead to God's Wrath, Turn U.S. Into Sodom, Watch Wing Right. http://www.rightwingwatch.org/post/pat-robertson-gay-marriage-will-lead-to-gods-wrath-turn-us-into-sodom/ (accessed on November 12, 2018).

14. Same Sex Marriage, Top Dissertations, https://top-dissertations.com/ (accessed on August 15, 2017).

15. Karlyn Bowman, Eleanor O'Neil, and Heather Sims, Public Opinion on Same-Sex Marriage: Anatomy of a Change, AEI. Poll Report. aei.org/wp-content/uploads/2015/06/Same-Sex-Marriage-Special-Report_June-2015.pdf (accessed on December 15, 2018).

16. Polling Data is taken from Brewer and Wilcox's article "Trends: Same-Sex Marriage and Civil Unions" which cites the polling data from the Roper Center at the University of Connecticut, The Polling Report, and the websites of the poll sponsors (Brewer & Wilcox, 2005, 606).

17. heterosexual couples and they will be able to enjoy the .... https://www.coursehero.com/file/p51j7b9/heterosexual-couples-and-they-will-be-able-to-enjoy-the-same-lifestyle-that-a/ (accessed on June 15, 2019).

18. Health care coverage options for same-sex couples .... https://www.health care.gov/married-same-sex-couples-and-the-marketplace/ (accessed on June 16, 2019).

19. Same Sex Marriage - Top-Dissertations.com. https://top-dissertations.com/essays/Sociology/same-sex-marriage/ (accessed July 1, 2019).

20. Kerri Anne Renzulli, What the Same-Sex Marriage Ruling Means for Couples' Finances, Money. http://money.com/

money/3933620/same-sex-marriage-money/ (accessed September 12, 2018).

21. Up with Worship! - Crosswalk.com. https://www.crosswalk.com/church/worship/up-with-worship-11551783.html (accessed on April 25, 2019).

22. Somerville, The Case Against "Same-Sex Marriage," su-pra note 199 (See, e.g., Margaret A. Somerville, The Case Against "Same-Sex Marriage": A Brief Submitted to the Standing Committee on Justice and Human Rights, at http://marriageinstitute.ca/ image-es/somerville.pdf (last visited April 29, 2003)

23. Robert P. George, in defense of natural law 139–53, 161–83 (1999) [hereinafter George, in defense of natural law]. d. at 140–41.

24. Same-Sex Marriage: Does It Meet with God's Approval .... https://www.ucg.org/the-good-news/same-sex-marriage-does-it-meet-with-gods-approval (February 12, 2018).

25. John-Henry Westen, Same-Sex Marriage a Health Risk Doctors Warn Parliamentarians, 2017, LifeSite. https://www.lifesitenews.com/news/same-sex-marriage-a-health-risk-doctors-warn-parliamentarians (accessed on December 20, 2017).

26. Public Health Ethics - NACCHO. https://www.naccho.org/programs/public-health-infrastructure/ethics (accessed on October 12, 2018).

27. Medical Downside of Homosexual Behavior. http://www.personal.psu.edu/glm7/m160.htm (accessed on August 12, 2017).

28. Timothy and Kathy Keller, *The Meaning of Marriage: Facing the Complexities of Commitment with the Wisdom of God* (New York, NY: Dutton, 2008).

29. Pam Belluck, Massachusetts Rejects Bill to Eliminate Gay Marriage, N.Y. TIMES, September 15, 2005, at A14. https://www.nytimes.com/2005/09/15/us/massachusetts-rejects-bill-to-eliminate-gay-marriage.html (accessed on May 18, 2019).

30. Gerard V. Bradley, Stand and Fight: Don't take gay marriage lying down, 55 NAT'L REV. 14, (2003).

CHAPTER 9. WHAT'S CONTROLLING YOUR MIND?

1. JNeverBeGameOver's, NeverBeGameOver's Steam Group. https://www.reddit.com/r/NeverBeGameOver/ (accessed on April 1, 2018).

2. Robert Smith, Jr., *Doctrine that Dance* (Nashville, TN: B & H Publishing, 2008), 53.

3. The Qualities of a Godly Mate, Bible.org. https://Bible.org/seriespage/12-qualities-godly-mate (accessed on January 18, 2019).

4. Challenges for the 21st Century Church, Global Christian Center. https://globalchristiancenter.com/administrative-leadership/church-leadership/25079-challenges-for-the-21st-century-church (accessed on May 20, 2019).

5. Bill Haley, Understanding the Gen Z Mindset, Allied Pixel, https://www.alliedpixel.com/2017/11/understanding-gen-z-mindset/ (accessed on August 23, 2018).

6. Atheism Doubles Among Generation Z - Barna Group. https://www.barna.com/research/atheism-doubles-among-generation-z/ (accessed May 12, 2018).

7. Ed Bahler Conquering the Challenges of the 21st Century Church, The Aspen Group. https://www.aspengroup.com/blog/conquering-the-challenges-of-the-21st-century-church (accessed on March 09, 2018).

8. *Word Pictures in the New Testament* (Nashville: Broadman, 1931), 89.

9. Jaelene Hinkle left off U.S. 2019 Women's World Cup roster. https://sports.yahoo.com/jaelene-hinkle-uswnt-world-cup-roster-lgbtq-pride-jersey-194321103.html (accessed on July 2, 2018).

10. Timothy Williams and Elizabeth Dias, United Methodists Tighten Ban on Same-Sex Marriage and Gay Clergy, https://www.nytimes.com/2019/02/26/us/united-methodists-vote.html (accessed on March 26, 2019).

11. Ricky Moore, *My Passion for Preaching* (Salt Lake City, UT: Aardvark Publishing Company, 2008), 245.

CHAPTER 10. GETTING USED TO YOUR BLESSINGS

1. Top 10 Secrets Behind Successful Marriages — CharimaNews. https://www.charismanews.com/opinion/43568-top-10-secrets-behind-successful-marriages?start=8 (accessed July 16, 2019).

2. T. D. Jakes, *Loose That Man and Let Him Go* (Minneapolis, Minnesota: Bethany House, 2003).

3. Enda McDonagh, *Love: The Westminster Dictionary of Christian Theology.* Eds. Alan Richardson and John Bowden (Philadelphia: The Westminster Press, 1983), 34.

4. Lectionary Commentaries - The African American Lectionary. http://www.theafricanamericanlectionary.org/

PopupLectionaryReading.asp?LRID=260 (accessed on January 23, 2018).

5. Jean M. Twenge, Ph.D., and W. Keith Campbell, Ph.D. *The Narcissism Epidemic: Living in the Age of Entitlement* (New York: Free Press, 2009), 221.

6. Smiley Blanton, M. D., *Love or Perish* (New York: NY: Simon & Schuster, 1956).

7. Charles R. Swindoll, *The Finishing Touch* (Dallas, TX: Word Publishing, 1994), 58–59.

8. Marriage Enrichment, Lectionary Commentary, http://www.theafricanamericanlectionary.org/PopupLectionaryReading.asp?LRID=260, (July 14, 2018).

9. Candace Crabtree, 20 Scripture Verses to Pray for Your Marriage, Crosswalk.com. https://www.crosswalk.com/slideshows/20-verses-to-Scripture-verses-pray-for-your-marriage.html (accessed on July 7, 2019).

10. The Conditions of a Good Marriage: Secular and Religious Views, Sample Thesis. https://asamplethesis.blogspot.com/2011/06/conditions-of-good-marriage-secular-and.html (accessed on March 17, 2019).

11. Maximum Marriage with Minimum Misery - Love Worth Finding .... https://www.oneplace.com/ministries/love-worth-finding/read/articles/maximum-marriage-with-minimum-misery-9853.html (accessed April 23, 1918).

12. PROBLEM Archives - MARVINSPIRE FITNESS. https://marvinspirefitness.com/tag/problem/(accessed on June 30, 2019).

13. Lectionary Commentaries - The African American Lectionary. http://www.theafricanamericanlectionary.org/

PopupLectionaryReading.asp?LRID=260 (accesses on January 26, 2019).

14. William Barclay, *The Letter to the Corinthians: The New Daily Study Bible* (Louisville: Westminster John Knox, 2002), 147–148.

15. Cindy and Steve Wright, "Loving Extravagantly—Marriage Message #235." Online location: http://www. marriagemissions.com/ loving-extravagantly-marriage-message-235/ (accessed on March 25, 2019).

16. Conley Bayless, Ten Commandments for your marriage, Marriagecapsule https://www.marriagecapsule.com/ten-commandments-ftroor-your-marriage/# (accessed on May 25, 2019).

CHAPTER 11. THE JOY OF GOOD CHARACTER

1. Top 10 Secrets Behind Successful Marriages — CharimaNews. https://www.charismanews.com/opinion/43568-top-10-secrets-behind-successful-marriages?start=8 (accessed July 16, 2019).

2. Blaine J. Flowers, *Beyond the Myth of Marital Happiness* (San Francisco, CA: Jossey-Bass, Inc., 2000), 72.

3. Pastor John K. Jenkins, https://www.kingofreads.com/pastor-responds-to-letter-from-lesbian-who-called-him-out-on-homophobic-sermon/ (accessed on February 27, 2019)

4. John Piper, "It Is Better to Marry Than to Burn with Passion, https://www.desiringgod.org/interviews/it-is-better-to-marry-than-to-burn-with-passion-what-does-this-mean (April 7, 2019).

5. Michael Green, The Model of the Apostle Paul, https://
   billygraham.org/decision-magazine/may-2007/the-model-of-
   the-apostle-paul/ (accessed on April 6, 2018).

CHAPTER 12. REMEMBER THE LORD
IN THE DAYS OF YOUR YOUTH

1. 4 Keys to Wise Living | Keep Believing Ministries. https://
   www.keepbelieving.com/sermon/4-keys-to-wise-living/
   (accessed March 31, 2019). Kimberly R. Davis, *Reclaiming
   Generation* (Richland, VA: KPG Publishing and Education,
   2013), 43-60.

2. Michael Adamse, *Anniversary: A Love Story* (Deerfield Beach,
   FL: Health Communication, Inc., 1998), 175.

3. Review of studies on infidelity - IPEDR. http://www.ipedr.
   com/vol19/34-ICAMS2011-A10054.pdf (accessed on January
   26, 2018).

4. Paul Coleman, PSY.D., *Spouse* (Avon, Mass.: Adams Media,
   2009), 182–183.

5. Infidelity Statistics - Truth About Deception. https://www.
   truthaboutdeception.com/cheating-and-infidelity/stats-
   about-infidelity.html (accessed on May 18, 2018).

6. Types of Infidelity, https://www.divorceknowledgebase.com/
   blog/types-of-infidelity/ (accessed on January 26, 2018).

7. TRUTH ABOUT DECEPTION-Facts and Statistics About
   Infidelity, https://www.truthaboutdeception.com/cheating-
   and-infidelity/stats-about-infidelity.html (accessed on
   February 23, 2019).

8. Drigotas, S. M. S., C. Annette; Gentilia, Tiffany. 1999. An in-vestment model prediction of dating infidelity. *Journal of Personality and Social Psychology.* 77(3):15.

9. Review of studies on infidelity - IPEDR. http://www.ipedr.com/vol19/34-ICAMS2011-A10054.pdf (accessed on May 18, 2018).

10. Paul Coleman, PSY.D., *Spouse* (Avon, Mass.: Adams Media, 2009), 181.

11. Stats About Cheating & Relationships the Hard Truth. http://loveengineer.com/cheating-relationships-stats-men-women/ (accessed on May 18, 2018).

12. Joanne Rogers, to forgive A Cheating Husband, https://worriedlovers.com/how-to-forgive-cheating-husband/?s1=&s2=&s3=&s4=bing (accessed January 29, 2019).

13. Gordon, K. C., Baucom, D. H., & Snyder, D. K. 2004. An integrative intervention for promoting recovery from extramarital affairs. *Journal of Marital and Family Therapy,* 30:33.

14. . Men who have affairs are more likely to do so for sexual .... https://www.coursehero.com/file/p5tjfim1/Men-who-have-affairs-are-more-likely-to-do-so-for-sexual-excitement-and-variety/ (accessed on January 15, 2019).

15. 10 Reasons David Is Called "A Man After God's Own Heart .... http://ronedmondson.com/2014/04/10-reasons-david-is-called-a-man-after-gods-own-heart.html (May 12, 2019).

16. *Men of the Bible devotional* (Uhrichsville, OH; Babour Books, 2015), 72.

CHAPTER 13 WALKING WORTHY OF WHO I AM

1. What does the Bible say about transformation? https://www. gotquestions.org/Bible-transformation.html (accessed June 1, 2019).

2. Bulletin – USGA. https://us.tjc.org/bulletin/ (accessed on April 29, 2019).

3. Are younger generation more accepting of same-sex marriage, are younger generations more accepting of same sex. Debate.com. https://www.debate.org/opinions/are-younger-generations-more-accepting-of-same-sex-marriage-because-they-are-not-as-heavily-involved-with- religion?nsort=6&ysort=5&_escaped_fragment_=&_escaped_fragment_=&_escaped_fragment_=&_escaped_fragment_= (accessed on April 25, 2017).

4. Can same-sex marriage help save the institution of .... https:// www.debate.org/opinions/can-same-sex-marriage-help-save-the-institution-of-marriage#! (accessed May 1, 2018).

5. JA Van der Ven, *Formation of the Moral Self* (Grand Rapids, MI: Wm. B. Eerdmans, 1998), 181.

6. Atheism Doubles Among Generation Z, Barna https://www. barna.com/research/atheism-doubles-among-generation-z/ (accessed on February 14, 2018). 8.

7. TFP Student Action, 10 Reasons Why Homosexual "Marriage" is Harmful and Must be Opposed, https://www. tfpstudentaction.org/blog/10-reasons-why-homosexual-marriage-is-harmful-and-must-be-opposed (May 5, 2019).

8. Roxanne Stone, Barna's Editor in Chief, Who is Gen Z? - Barna Group. https://www.barna.com/who-is-gen-z/ (accessed January 30, 2018)).

9. Barna Study Finds Gen Z Is the Least Christian Generation in American History, Black Christian News Network One. http://blackchristiannews.com/2018/01/barna-study-finds-gen-z-is-the-least-christian-generation-in-american-history/ accessed January 30, 2018).

10. Generation Z more Conservative than Millennials on Gay Is-sues, The Data Lounge, https://www.datalounge.com/thread/17664485-generation-z-more-conservative-than-millennials-on-gay-issues (accessed on April 25, 2019).

11. Changing Views of Same-Sex Marriage, The Pew Center, https://www.people-press.org/2015/06/08/section-1-changing-views-of-same-sex-marriage/ (accessed on May 30, 2019).

12. But I'm Nothing Like the Proverbs 31 Woman .... https://proverbs31.org/read/devotions/full-post/2019/04/25/but-im-nothing-like-the-proverbs-31-woman (accessed on September 14, 2018).

13. Earl Radmacher, Ronald B. Allen, and H. Wayne House, *Nelson's New Illustrations Bible Commentary* (Nashville, TN: Thomas Nelson, Inc., 1999), 1448–1449.

14. Greenwood Hills LIFE: August 2009. https://greenwoodhillslife.blogspot.com/2009/08/ (accessed on May 16, 2019).

15. Trinity United Methodist Church NON-PROFIT ORGANIZATION .... http://n.b5z.net/i/u/10176465/f/FEBRUARY2015NEWSLETERPDF.pdf (accessed on Trinity United Methodist Church NON-PROFIT ORGANIZATION .... http://n.b5z.net/i/u/10176465/f/FEBRUARY2015NEWSLETERPDF.pdf18, 2019).

CHAPTER 14 SOMETHING IN THE STRUGGLES

1. Covenant Marriage - Definition, Examples, Cases, Processes. https://legaldictionary.net/covenant-marriage/ (accessed May 1, 2019).